City Guide
Tel Aviv

Open

How to use City Guide Tel Aviv

City Guide Tel Aviv divides the city into six primary areas. Each area includes a variety of locations – restaurants, cafes, bars, clubs, designers, boutiques and hotels, as well as texts about the areas and relevant maps.

Each location is featured in the relevant area where one can find photographs and descriptions, as well as an address and phone number. The area code for Tel Aviv is 03 inside the country and (972 – 3) if calling from abroad.

Each location is shown as a circled number on the relevant area map which is intended to give a rough idea of location and proximity rather than a precise position.

In the last section of the book one can find contact information for the galleries, museums and cultural centers of Tel Aviv and an index featuring complete information, such as fax numbers and websites for the different locations.

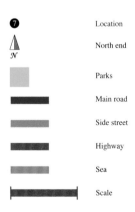

❼	Location
	North end
	Parks
	Main road
	Side street
	Highway
	Sea
	Scale

Introduction to Tel Aviv-Jaffa

The first edition of *Time Out Tel Aviv* rolled off the presses toward the end of 2002. The timing seemed a bit odd – the intifada was raging and unemployment was at an all-time high. Suicide bombings were a regular occurrence in Tel Aviv. One of the hottest pick up spots in town for twentysomething university graduates was the queue at the unemployment office. But just like its older sisters, *Time Out London* and *Time Out New York*, the Tel Aviv edition was all about celebrity parties, chic lounge bars, fashionable restaurants, edgy theatre performances, cinema and gay and lesbian events. Anyone flipping through the glossy pages would be hard-pressed to find evidence that Israel was in the midst of a crisis. When people say Tel Aviv is a city that never sleeps, they're not just talking about the exciting nightlife. They're talking about an attitude and a culture. The fact is that Tel Aviv's cultural life and nightlife thrived and prospered even during the most difficult months of political and economic upheaval. Nothing can interfere with the palpable sense of joie de vivre in this vibrant, endlessly fascinating city. Today it is better than ever – energetic, self-confident and hedonistic. Tel Aviv's residents have an ongoing romance with their city, and first-time visitors are quickly seduced as well – once they see past the urban grit. Soon to celebrate its 100th anniversary, Tel Aviv is a Mediterranean city with a Levantine flavor and a European twist. It has a liberal, laid-back atmosphere, a beach-oriented summer culture and lots of beautiful people. The city hosts one of the largest annual gay pride parades in the world, commonly attracting over 100,000 participants and spectators; its cafe culture is an integral part of the city's character and its restaurants have attracted the attention of prominent international critics. There are dozens of art galleries, a critically acclaimed opera company and a world-renowned symphony orchestra, conducted by Zubin Mehta. There are around one dozen theaters, from Habimah Theater, Israel's national theater, to fringe theater; per capita, Tel Aviv has one of the highest numbers of theater attendees in the world. With the exception of two major holidays, Tel Aviv is a 24-hour city. There are dozens of restaurants, clubs, pubs and lounge bars that hum with energy from three o'clock in the morning until dawn, when windsurfers, joggers and yoga practitioners appear on the beach and the night owls head home to sleep. Whatever the time, whatever the day, there is always something to do, see and experience in Tel Aviv.

History of Tel Aviv-Jaffa - A joint municipality since the early 1950s, Tel Aviv and Jaffa are, respectively, the newest and oldest cities in the Middle East. Founded 1,500 years ago, Jaffa is in fact one of the oldest cities in the world: When European cities like Prague and Budapest were founded, Jaffa was already a thriving port city. Nearly a millennium later, Jaffa gave birth to Tel Aviv. The first pioneers of the modern Zionist movement landed at Jaffa port toward the end of the 19th century, when it was still part of the Ottoman Empire, with many settling in the city alongside the long-established Sephardic Jewish community. In the mid-1880s prominent members of that community established the neighborhoods of Neve Tzedek and Neve Shalom on Jaffa's outskirts, later to be incorporated into what is now South Tel Aviv. In 1909, some of those Zionist pioneers famously gathered on a beach just outside Jaffa and established Ahuzat Bayit, a community that was later re-named Tel Aviv (Hill of Spring), after the Hebrew title of Theodore Herzl's seminal book, *Altneuland*. From 1909-1932, Tel Aviv was a sleepy little village that developed slowly, in fits and stops. The predominant architectural style was eclectic – a mixture of Levantine, Central European and Oriental influences – and the street planning somewhat haphazard. At the beginning of the 1920s, two major events occurred and determined the city's future: Jaffa's commercial center moved to Tel Aviv, following violent confrontations between the Jewish and Arab communities of Jaffa; and Sir Patrick Geddes created a modern urban plan for Tel Aviv, based on the Garden City concept. Geddes was a visionary who planned the city so that it would answer its residents' spiritual needs and their material needs. He took into account all sorts of factors, ranging from climate and social structure to income. He believed in fostering human interaction by bringing people together naturally in public places, such as squares, parks and streets; he did not believe in separating the commercial center from the residential areas, lest the former become ghost towns during non-working hours. Residential buildings were to be low-rise, airy, aesthetically pleasing and inexpensive. Geddes was one of the foremost promoters of the Garden City – one that maintains a connection with nature. Most of all, he believed in quality of life and natural evolution. Geddes planned a city for up to 100,000 residents, but today the core of Tel Aviv is home to more than 300,000; metropolitan Tel Aviv has a population of 600,000 and Greater Tel Aviv is home to approximately 1 million residents. While the growth did occur organically, as per Geddes' plan, he did not reckon with the sheer number of cars and buses that would one day ply the city's roads – particularly during business hours, when people from the suburbs of Greater Tel Aviv come into the city to work. As a result there are often traffic jams that create clouds of pollution. Despite visible neglect, the basic vision of a livable urban space has held: Tel Aviv is a social city, a city that has evolved organically and one that

is lined with tree shaded boulevards and dotted with green parks. It is a vibrant city that throbs with energy; there is clearly an ongoing struggle between Geddes' plan and the needs of a 21st century metropolis, but so far the balance between preservation and modernization has held.

The illustrated story of Tel Aviv in architecture - From Neve Tzedek in southern Tel Aviv to the high-rises along the Ayalon Highway, the history of Tel Aviv is told in its architecture. That history can roughly be divided into 20-year periods: the two decades before Geddes' plan was implemented; the International style decades from 1932 to the early 1950s; the boxy, vaguely Soviet style of the following two decades; the misguided power architecture of the 1970s and 1980s; and the sleek, modern, Norman Foster look that has prevailed from the early 1990s to the present. Each style reflects the unique historical and economic conditions of its time. Throughout southern Tel Aviv – particularly in the Florentine area and along Allenby Street – there are many examples of old edifices dating back to the years immediately before and after World War I. These buildings are characterized by an Ottoman interpretation of romanticized neo-classical influences, with lots of carved pillars, Oriental arches, tiny Romeo-and-Juliet balconies and other rococo flourishes. They were built before Geddes' plan was implemented, and before the massive influx of refugees who fled Hitler's Germany in the 1930s. They are not quite Levantine, not quite European – not quite anything specific, really. And yet they are romantic, and they evoke a sense of nostalgia. Even when they were first constructed, however, they were not modern – nor were they particularly practical to accommodate the residents of a rapidly growing city, which is what Tel Aviv became, quite suddenly and due to unique historical circumstances – the massive influx of refugees from Nazi Europe. The architects who designed the residences for all those newly arrived refugees were trained in Germany and were influenced by the Bauhaus School of Design founded in Weimar in 1919 by Walter Gropius. Its signature modernist style was enormously influential throughout the world. As soon as the Nazis came to power, they closed the school and several Jewish architects who were influenced by the style ended up in Tel Aviv, which became the blank canvas upon which they built the first – and only – Bauhaus city. Starting from 1932, until the first two years of the 1950s, an estimated 5,000 low-rise residences in the International, or Modern, Style were constructed in Tel Aviv and Jaffa. It is this style that has become Tel Aviv's most visible characteristic. All over the city there are low-rise buildings with elegant curves, square balconies, porthole windows. They are otherwise remarkably simple – free of any excess decoration. Once, they symbolized all that was modern about Tel Aviv. They were clean, sparkling

and new. And then they aged rather rapidly – helped along by neglect and the salty winds of the Mediterranean. Then, toward the end of the 1980s, their aesthetic and historical value was recognized. In 2003 UNESCO declared Tel Aviv a world heritage site and there is a new trend to renovate and preserve the Bauhaus buildings. Many – perhaps most – are still neglected, largely because they have been designated heritage buildings and are thus expensive to renovate. But there are many beautifully refurbished buildings all over the city. The style that was once the pinnacle of modernity has become a sort of modern antique and Tel Aviv is now frequently referred to as a "living museum" of Bauhaus architecture. Interspersed with the Bauhaus buildings are many charmless, boxy structures that evoke images of suburban Stalinist Moscow. These were constructed during the 1950s and 1960s, when Israel was a struggling young state with a rapidly growing population and limited financial means. Function was the primary factor in planning these structures, with form a very distant second. They are still very much in use, though age has lent them little charm. But they are a part of the landscape and also a part of the city's history. And then came muscular architecture of the 1970s, known as Brutalism – from the French *béton brut*, or "raw concrete" – in which style many public buildings and monuments are built. The most prominent and best examples are City Hall – reminiscent of Le Corbusier's Unite d'Habitation in Marseille – and the Tel Aviv museums; some bad examples are Dizengoff Center, the pedestrian bridge over Dizengoff Square and the unfinished eyesore of Kikar Atarim at the foot of Ben Gurion Boulevard. The city underwent major changes during those decades. Prominent among them is the beachfront promenade, for which the legendary mayor Shlomo "Chich" Lahat is best known. The promenade, which is currently undergoing renovations, extends from Jaffa all the way up to the Hayarkon Park, and it is much beloved by Tel Avivians. One of the city's great, simple pleasure is a leisurely stroll or bicycle ride up and down the promenade, along the Mediterranean coast, from ancient Jaffa to the green expanses of the park in the north; the recent renovations made this uninterrupted journey possible. On Saturday afternoons the promenade is packed with strolling couples and families, street artists, hucksters and musicians. The promenade is a major gathering place and a center of this Mediterranean city's life. Over the last 20 years or so, bland office buildings and apartment towers have sprung up all over the city. They reflect its rapid westernization and its increasing importance as a high-tech and business center. There are those who believe Tel Aviv is in a period of major transformation, and that the result will be the dwarfing of the old structures. But the desire to preserve the city's character is strong. Tel

Avivians love their city and want it to remain a livable place, so chances are that a middle ground between modernization and preserving the past will be found – especially given the large number of preservationists who work at the municipality.

Lifestyle - Tel Avivians live much of their lives outdoors. This is partly because of the climate – guaranteed sunshine for most of the year and a short, mild winter – and partly because the city's design naturally pulls people to gather in public spaces. Outdoor cafes are an extension of this outdoor lifestyle, and the cafe culture is one of the city's defining characteristics. It is almost impossible to walk for more than 50 meters anywhere in Tel Aviv without coming across a cafe. They line the main streets and dot the side streets. Everyone has a favorite cafe, a neighborhood hangout – whether it's a no-frills veteran joint like Tamar's on Sheinkin or one of the sleek, trendy new places that seem to pop up in a new location every other day. Sometimes it's as though the city is saturated in cafes, but then again none of them seems to lack for customers. Tel Avivians gather at cafes to read the morning newspapers with their coffee, to work on their laptops (free wireless internet connections are the norm), to hold business meetings, to gossip with friends. It is completely acceptable to linger over a coffee for hours; whereas in New York a waiter might hint it's time to be moving on by "dropping the bill" on the table, that kind of attitude is simply unheard of in Tel Aviv. For a visitor who wants to soak up the local culture, a cafe is the ideal place to start – and stay. Much of this book is about Tel Aviv's fabulous nightlife. It is anarchistic, cutting edge and hedonistic, but neither threatening nor intimidating. All the intimidating factors that characterize nightlife in London and New York – the aggressive posing, the hostile bouncers, the pushy drunkards – are completely absent in Tel Aviv. The nightlife starts late – the lounge bars open around 10 p.m., but don't start to fill up until at least an hour later. The discos and clubs usually open at midnight. And there are many restaurants that are open 24 hours. It wasn't always like this – the truth is that Tel Aviv's nightlife really started to take off during the late 1990s. But since then it hasn't looked back. Famous DJs frequently fly in from London or Amsterdam to perform on Thursday night, the opening night of the Israeli weekend, and then fly back home in time for the Friday night scene. The lounge bars, clubs and restaurants of Tel Aviv compete quite easily with those in New York or London. First-time visitors frequently express surprise at discovering the level of sophistication in Tel Aviv, but for locals it is taken as a matter of course. Tel Aviv grew up very quickly over the past decade or so, and few people remember the days – just over two decades ago – when it was a quiet, provincial backwater. There are plenty of lectures, art galleries, concerts and dance performances. There is no shortage of creative local artists, either. All over the city, on any given night, there are poetry readings, experimental theater performances, live avant-garde jazz by local and international artists, and performances of local pop, rock and folk music. The city draws up-and-coming artists from all over the country, and it buzzes with creative energy. Another thriving industry is that of book publishing, with approximately 13,000 new titles being released annually in Israel.

Advice for travelers - Tel Aviv is a laid-back city that is easy to enjoy. The people are neither particularly effusive toward visitors nor hostile – they're just mellow, relaxed and straightforward. There is no urban violence in Tel Aviv, which is why women and children feel completely safe wandering the streets alone late at night. Muggings are unheard of. Simple, fresh, tasty and inexpensive food is available at any cafe, as is excellent espresso. Hardly anyone drinks the stuff, but if your definition of coffee is the American style drip brew, then ask for "filter coffee." Taxis are not expensive – an average journey within city limits will cost between three and five US dollars. The driver is required by law to turn on the meter and it is not customary to tip. It is customary to tip waiters – usually around 12 percent for a meal, although most people leave two shekels for a coffee, which usually costs 8 shekels. During the hot, humid summer months most young Tel Avivians wear a variation on baggy trousers, loose tank tops and flips. Suits and ties are practically unheard of, except maybe for attorneys arguing a case in court. During the cooler winter months people do dress up a bit more, but basically Tel Aviv is a very casual city – jeans and a nice shirt are appropriate for just about any occasion, even a wedding or a celebrity party. Nobody will look at you strangely if you prefer to dress up a bit more, but it's not necessary.

Consider this book your guide to approaching the city as the locals do – with a lighthearted, open-minded and relaxed attitude.

North end

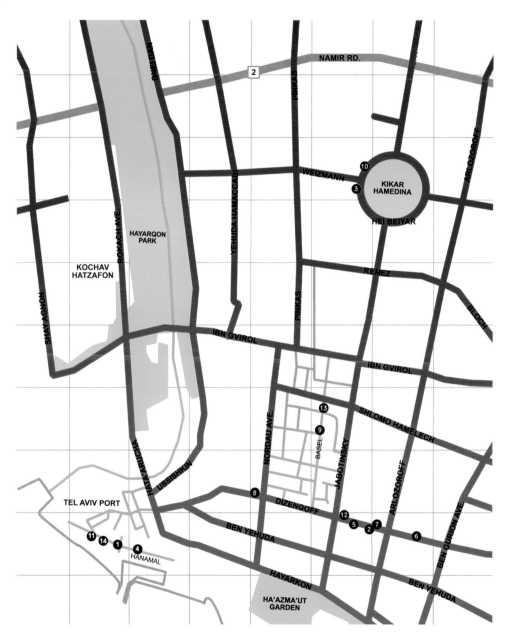

NAMIR RD.

2

PINKAS

ARLOZOROFF

BNEI DAN

YEHUDA HAMACCABI

WEIZMANN

10

KIKAR
HAMEDINA

3

HEI BEIYAR

ROKACH AVE.

HAYARQON
PARK

KOCHAV
HATZAFON

REMEZ

SHAY AGNON

PINKAS

BLOCH

IBN GVIROL

IBN GVIROL

SHLOMO HAMELECH

13

NORDAU AVE.

9

BASEL

JABOTINSKY

HATAYARUCHA

USSISHKIN

8

DIZENGOFF

ARLOZOROFF

TEL AVIV PORT

12 5 2 7

6

BEN YEHUDA

BEN GURION AVE.

11 14 1 4

HANAMAL

HAYARKON

BEN YEHUDA

HA'AZMA'UT
GARDEN

300m

The north end of Tel Aviv is solidly bourgeois and Ashkenazi and feels far more influenced by Europe than the Middle East. It is quiet, green, prosperous and pleasantly dull. This is where the icons of upper middle class Tel Aviv are located – like Kikar Hamedina, with its European designer shops, Assuta Hospital, which is private and caters to the wealthy, and the Herzliya Gymnasium, one of the country's most prestigious high schools. This is possibly one of the last places in Israel where it is common to see elegantly dressed septuagenarian women, with bags that match their shoes, sitting in cafes and chatting in German or Hungarian – or in carefully enunciated, grammatically perfect, old-fashioned Hebrew. It is an aging neighborhood, although recently there has been an influx of young urban professionals who are looking for the closest thing to the suburbs within the big city. You can spot them easily: look for the thirtysomething couples – she with a perky blonde ponytail and he with a Montblanc pen in his shirt pocket – pushing a baby in a carriage and pulling a dog on a leash. Despite its socio-economic prestige, this area is not architecturally distinguished. Unlike the rest of Tel Aviv, the north end is not strongly characterized by the Modernist look and there are few noteworthy examples of International style low-rise residential buildings. There are, however, many examples of utilitarian-looking residences that were constructed in the 1960s and 1970s – especially around Yehuda Hamaccabi. The most prominent aesthetic characteristic of this area is the high concentration of green parks – especially Hayarkon Park, the jewel in the crown. The north end of Tel Aviv is also a major shopping area for upscale designer clothes – both local and imported. It has a high concentration of elegant – and expensive – boutiques, particularly on North Dizengoff and around Kikar Hamedina.

North Dizengoff, Basel Square and Kikar Hamedina - When fashionable Israelis with disposable income – or a sizable overdraft – go shopping, they usually head to North Dizengoff, Basel Square and Kikar Hamedina. Each has clusters of exclusive boutiques, with the types of designers varying from one area to the next. North Dizengoff is sometimes referred to as fashion row. This is where nearly all of Israel's most prominent homegrown designer boutiques are located. The local talent is quite impressive and often unique, ranging from elegant evening gowns to trendy club gear, with well-cut business suits and casual apparel a strong presence, as well. Several of the designers have won prestigious international fashion awards. There are also many bridal boutiques in this area. On Thursday, the most popular day to marry, stiffly gowned and carefully coiffed young women emerge in the afternoons from the boutiques to be photographed and filmed, before they enter the waiting car that will whisk them off to the ceremony. North Dizengoff is also a pleasant place to stroll, cafe hop and window shop. It is tree-and-bench lined and remarkably quiet in comparison with the southern stretch of the street. The shops around Basel Square are not quite as cutting-edge as those on North Dizengoff. There are a few boutiques that specialize in fashionable, expensive maternity and baby clothes and some branches of well-known Israeli designer boutiques. Otherwise, this is really more of a place to purchase accessories – from scented candles to imported Italian dishes and locally designed jewelry. And then there is Kikar Hamedina, the name that is synonymous with money. This circular "square" has the highest concentration of prestigious international name brands in the city, from Rolex and Bulgari to Ralph Lauren and Versace; in many ways, it resembles a big duty free shop. And indeed, Kikar Hamedina is the place where Israeli plutocrats who don't have time to hop over to Europe for a weekend shopping spree come to purchase their clothes and jewelry. Interestingly, because of a municipal zoning law there is only one cafe on Kikar Hamedina; the rest are clustered on the side streets that are like spokes sticking out from a wheel. Over the past few years, Kikar Hamedina has acquired an interesting reputation for class conflict. A few years ago the grassy circular park was nicknamed Bread Square after low-income protestors set up a squatters' camp there to protest cuts in welfare and housing benefits, at a time when unemployment was at a record high. The sit-in ended after several months, without achieving any tangible results – and it did not succeed in embarrassing away the shoppers, either. But there is a reminder of Israel's rapidly widening socio-economic gaps in the park's still-neglected appearance. This is one of Kikar Hamedina's strange characteristics: It is a place known for luxury and prestige, but it looks rather down at the heels. But soon the park will disappear. It is privately owned and plans are underway to make it the site of a luxury-housing complex, after the owner won a 20-year battle with the local residents and the municipality.

The North Port and Hayarkon Park - For years, Tel Aviv's North Port was a site of major urban blight. Recently it underwent a refurbishing and gentrification process and is now one of the most popular areas in the city to eat, shop, stroll and troll the nightlife. There are parts that still look like a port, with the apparatus for unloading ships' cargo left intact – although it is no longer used – and the leisure areas are built around them. This was a conscious decision, and the result is an interesting juxtaposition of modern, fashionable Tel Aviv with its recent past. The waterfront has a wooden boardwalk that is lined with cafes, restaurants and bars and the sections that are set back from the water are packed with some of the city's trendiest nightclubs. There is almost never a time when the port is empty of people. Joggers appear early in the morning, later on families and young couples come to stroll the boardwalk and stop for lunch at one of the pretty cafes. After dark the port becomes a major nightlife scene, with music spilling out the doors of the clubs and dance bars. A stroll from the north port up to Hayarkon Park, Israel's largest public park, is a uniquely Tel Aviv experience, and highly recommended – especially on a lazy Saturday afternoon. At nearly 4 kilometers square, Hayarkon Park rivals New York's Central Park in both size and beauty. Bicyclists traverse the path along the riverbank, families picnic on the tree-shaded grass and there are even regular cricket games between teams of ex-pat Indian diamond merchants and locals. It's a great, multi-cultural Israeli gathering place – magically peaceful and pleasant.The park features an aviary, a waterpark and an artificial lake. The whole area is well maintained by the municipality, and treated with an unusual degree of respect in a country where public spaces are often sadly abused.

Yehuda Hamaccabi - Yehuda Hamaccabi Boulevard and the surrounding streets were planned and built during the 1960s, as was Tel Aviv University. Prior to that, the city ended at Hayarkon Park. Like the rest of the north end, this is a prestigious, upper class neighborhood. The tree-lined boulevard is notable mostly for its cafes and the side streets for their quiet, very middle class atmosphere. There is not a lot to draw a visitor here, but it's a nice place to stroll or stop for a coffee if you find yourself in the neighborhood. This area really feels like a rather Germanic (some say it is reminiscent of Frankfurt), well-ordered suburb in the city. There are clusters of private homes with little gardens, for example – a sort of realization of the city's founders' vision of a "garden city."

Comme il faut house at the Tel Aviv port [1]

Bait Banamal, Hanger 26, Tel Aviv Port
Telephone (03) 5449211 – Restaurant Comme il faut
Telephone (03) 5444462 – Spa Coola
Telephone (03) 6025530 – Boutique Comme il faut

The comme il faut house is a light, airy and modern space that houses a restaurant, boutique and spa. Although the spa and boutique are targeted at women, the cafe is justifiably popular with everyone for its excellent food and superb waterfront setting. The boutique - comme il faut is one of the most prestigious design labels in Israel. The high quality garments are fashionable but not trendy, simultaneously comfortable and luxurious. They're a bit pricey by Israeli standards, but are well worth the investment. The female design team has a philosophy of designing for "real women," as evidenced in a recent catalogue that showed well-known local writers, academics and artists of all body shapes, sizes and ages modeling the clothes. The spa - coola continues the theme of catering to intelligent, well-rounded women. In addition to facials, massages and other standard spa services, coola offers workshops, including belly dancing and yoga retreats. It also hosts weekly seminars on a variety of subjects that focus on social and environmental awareness. The restaurant - there's really nothing one can say to detract from the comme il faut cafe at the port. The waterfront setting is beautiful and the food is reliably good. Chef Hadassah Wolf's philosophy of slow food, organic ingredients and careful, creative preparation is certainly a success. And there are nice little details, such as the cookie served with coffee. This is a lovely place to linger, especially during the long summer.

Shay Lahover [2]
203 Dizengoff Street
Telephone (03) 5233887

Shay Lahover's exquisite jewelry has earned him a well-deserved local and international reputation for top tier design. His work is frequently shown at prominent galleries and exhibitions both in Israel and abroad, garnering gushing reviews in prominent international fashion magazines. Nava Barak, then wife of former prime minister Ehud Barak, commissioned a 22 karat gold, emerald and ruby hamsa, a traditional Jewish good luck charm, for Hillary Clinton when she visited Israel. Lahover draws his ideas from various artistic genres, architecture and archaeology for a timeless yet modern look that adapts to the personality of the wearer. His richly crafted pieces are molded from 22 and 24 karat gold, combined with fine silver and platinum and inlaid with precious and semi-precious stones from diamonds to tanzanite. The handcrafted look is unmistakable; each piece looks utterly personal and unique. They are large yet delicate, and impossible to ignore.

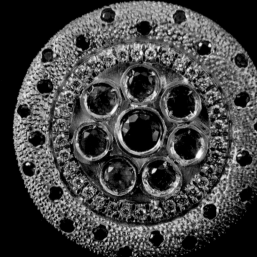

Metzada B-kikar [3]
60 Hei beiyar, Kikar Hamedina
Telephone (03) 5447766

Metzada Zeevi is an icon of style. She has a passion for fashion and is the exclusive importer of some of the most cutting-edge fashion names from Europe and the U.S. Her reputation extends well beyond Israel, to her many clients who live abroad and order their clothes directly from Metzada. The rich, varied collections at Metzada include Tony Mora boots, whimsically feminine Biya designs, Replay jeans and Charm and Luck bags. There are stunningly elegant evening gowns, deliciously feminine lingerie and irresistible accessories like BB Simon designer belts and shoes. There is also a wide range of exclusive home accessories, such as dishes, crystals and aromatic Votivo candles – much loved by stars like Madonna and Bruce Willis. With her impeccable fashion sense and individual style, Metzada shows her clients how to put everything together to create an individual look. For men, collections from Replay, Biya and additional designers are also available.

RESTAURANT
Mul Yam [4]
Hangar 24, Tel Aviv Port
Telephone (03) 5469920

When owner Shalom Maharovsky established Mul Yam (Facing the Sea) in 1995, he revolutionized the Israeli gastronomical scene, setting the standards against which all other restaurants are measured. Critics are unanimous in describing Mul Yam as the best restaurant in Israel. Mul Yam is the only Israeli restaurant to receive a star in the Guide Michelin. It is also listed by Les Grandes Tables du Monde as one of the 120 best restaurants in the world. Gault Millau gave it five stars - the highest possible ranking - in its Israel Guide. Chef Yoram Nitzan is regularly mentioned in the same breath as luminaries such as Daniel Boulud, Eric Ripert, Marc Veyrat and Marc Haeberlin. In fact, he trained with them all. The seasonal menu focuses on fish and seafood, but there are many land-based entrees as well. Nitzan uses a combination of local and imported ingredients - among the latter are delicacies such as lobsters from Canada, oysters from Brittany, black rice from China, berries from Provence and mushrooms from Tuscany. The extensive wine list includes Mul Yam's private label alongside a wide selection from the world's finest vintners. The desserts, too, are a study in excellence; the French-trained pastry chef's creations invariably evoke sighs of pleasure. The decor, with its blonde wood highlights and vases of fresh flowers, is simple, elegant and intimate. It complements the soothing view of the sea.

Yael Herman Gallery [5]

211 Dizengoff Street
Telephone (03) 5221816
Mobile 052 3676647

Yael Herman displays her jewelry designs in a stark white space that looks like an art gallery. In fact, she defines her unique and striking pieces as wearable art. The artist/designer creates contemporary jewelry in simple geometric forms composed of 18 karat gold, sterling silver, aluminum, stainless steel and diamonds, using a combination of modern technology and traditional craftsmanship. Each design, says Yael, is a three-dimensional sculpture that becomes part of the personality and spirit of the wearer. Herman's work has been featured at major international exhibitions, including COLLECT at London's Victoria and Albert Museum and the SOFA Art Fair at New York's Sienna Gallery. The latest collections include 23 karat gold leaf laminated necklaces and rings made of stainless steel and diamonds, with an open groove setting that allows the diamond to slide back and forth. It's rather mesmerizing to watch.

FASHION

Frida [6]
190 Dizengoff Street
Telephone (03) 5225151

Frida is a seriously talented designer who designs sophisticated, elegant garments. A graduate of Israel's prestigious Shenkar College of Fashion and Textiles, Frida was chosen from among 620 international contenders to compete in the prestigious Italian Mittelmoda Fashion Awards. She interned with Donna Karan in New York before returning to Tel Aviv to establish the boutique from which she sells her own designs. While her style is somewhat influenced by her experience with the famous American designer, Frida's collections are unmistakably unique. They are also comfortable, luxurious and flattering to a wide range of body types.

FASHION

Banot – Loulou Liam [7]
212 Dizengoff Street
Telephone (03) 5291175

The seasonal creations of fashion designer Loulou Liam use a unique vocabulary to define local symbolism – much like her logo "Banot" – girls. The new store, located in a former residential apartment on Dizengoff, challenges conventionalism by contrasting old and new to create a synergetic relation between user-space and product-place. The 2006 collection is a clear manifestation of Loulou's personal style, combining monochromatic textiles with silver and tanned-gold jewelry. Loulou creates a womanly silhouette that accentuates the vocal, the sexy and the feminine, with a taut line and rough urban feel. The store also introduces "Second Skin" – a new line of lingerie, featuring sheer camisoles and underwear in breathable cotton with pontelle patterns that evoke a fresh vintage look.

Fabiani [8]

280 Dizengoff Street
Telephone (03) 6025569

At Fabiani the atmosphere falls somewhere between sophisticated boutique and art gallery. Owner Diana Churges searches the world for unique clothes, shoes and accessories for her cosmopolitan and self-confident female clientele. The women who shop at Fabiani are most emphatically not interested in fashion for the masses. They have mature taste, and are searching for those rare items that are strikingly unique, complementing the wearer's personal style without overwhelming it. There are no trendy items or mainstream fashion brands. Rather, there is a constantly changing collection of wearable art that is almost impossible to find anywhere else. The special quality of items is apparent in the unconventional cut, whimsical details and unusual materials. Ms. Churges emphasizes that she chooses fashion for women who appreciate creative avant-garde but also demand comfortable clothes suitable for all situations.

Daniella Lehavi [9]

34 Basel Street
Telephone (03) 5440573
35 Sheinkin Street
Telephone (03) 6294044

When chic Israeli women are looking for high quality shoes and bags, they go to one of the seven Daniella Lehavi boutiques in the greater Tel Aviv area. The Swiss-born designer's shoes, bags and leather accessories are created with an eye to clean lines and a merging of form and function that are immensely appealing to women with style and - let's face it - a bit of disposable income. Lehavi's designs are not inexpensive, but they are well worth the investment. These are products that are made to last, and since the designs are classic there's no need to worry about them falling out of fashion. The knowledgeable and helpful staff invariably ask what your needs are: Is it a bag for work? Do you carry a laptop computer? Do you want an inside pocket for your mobile phone, or do you prefer a little pouch that clips onto the strap? Take your time browsing and consulting with the salespeople - they don't pressure their buyers.

Blue Bandana [10]

52 Hei beiyar, Kikar Hamedina
Telephone (03) 6021686

Located in prestigious northern Tel Aviv, Blue Bandana sells beautiful, unique home accessories to people with excellent taste. This small, stylish shop stocks an eclectic collection of handpicked items from all over the globe, with many designed exclusively for Blue Bandana. The stock is constantly updated, making each visit – and yes, there will be more than one - a pleasant journey of discovery. Ceramic dishes painted in deep, bold, difficult-to-achieve colors are carefully stacked on the industrial style metal shelves that line the otherwise minimalist white space. Items from Blue Bandana are regularly featured in the pages of the country's most prestigious newspapers and magazines, invariably with a gushing description of their aesthetic appeal. A visit to Blue Bandana is frequently the catalyst for an epiphany: Suddenly, you discover how many things you lack. And you understand that you really, really need them.

Agadir - Bar Burger [11]

3 Hata'arucha Street, Tel Aviv Port
Telephone (03) 5444045
2 Nachalat Binyamin Street
Telephone (03) 5104442

Agadir's huge, juicy gourmet hamburgers are probably the best in town. Given that the town is Tel Aviv, it should come as no surprise that the care and thought invested in those burgers is equally reflected in the decor. The tiled floors, warm yellow lighting and heavy wooden bar create a welcoming, slightly nostalgic - yet modern - atmosphere. Located at the old north port, with its many lounge bars and clubs, Agadir Hotel is open until 6 a.m. - making it an excellent place to refuel after a late night out. During non-vampire hours, Agadir Hotel is popular with everyone - from families to business people. The bar is well stocked, the chips are crispy and so are the salads. The veggie burger is a treat, too.

CAFE
Cafe Michal [12]
230 Dizengoff Street
Telephone (03) 5230236

Michal is one of the standout cafes in the North Dizengoff area. The magazines that decide and identify all that is fashionable regularly include it in their annually published lists of the best cafes in Tel Aviv. It's also a popular meeting place for some of the country's best-known young actors, writers and musicians. Ensconced on the corner of Jabotinsky and Dizengoff, Cafe Michal seduces passersby with its eclectic, cozy, upscale bohemian decor. The well-considered menu features delicious homemade soups, upscale cafe cuisine that always pleases the palate and buttery little homemade cookies to accompany your perfectly prepared Italian coffee.

CAFE
Cafe Ashtor [13]
37 Basel Street
Telephone (03) 5465318

Wrapped around one of the corners of Basel Square, Cafe Ashtor is sun-warmed during the winter and pleasantly breezy during the summer. This unpretentious, classically Tel Aviv cafe has a cozy neighborhood atmosphere, largely due to the near-constant presence of the friendly, down-to-earth owners. Basel may be lined with trendier or more expensive cafes, but none has the homey feel of the veteran Ashtor. The neighborhood regulars know this and wouldn't dream of drinking their morning cappuccino anywhere else. First-time visitors feel instantly comfortable at Ashtor - and soon they too become regulars.

Whisky a Go Go [14]
3 Hata'arucha Street, Tel Aviv Port
Telephone (03) 5440633

Among Tel Aviv's many legendary nightspots, Whisky a Go Go currently ranks amongst the very hottest. The multi-story mega lounge bar is where Israel's most famous musicians, models, athletes and actors go to eat, drink and then dance into the early hours. This is the first stop for a Tel Avivian who knows the nightlife scene and wants to impress visitors from abroad. Whisky a Go Go is a very good lounge bar that evolves from chic dining spot to throbbing dance bar as the night progresses. Many people come to eat a light dinner with friends in the earlier hours, then stay on to drink, socialize and listen to music. After midnight, the excellent DJs crank up the volume and the energy levels go off the charts. The late night scene is pretty wild. Crowds gather at the entrance, space inside is at a premium and the door people do become selective. At that point, it often helps to be beautiful and/or famous. Once inside, the senses are pleasantly overwhelmed by the not-quite-over-the-top decor, which is vaguely reminiscent of a 19th-century New Orleans brothel. The red lighting and red button-leather couches combine to create a flattering light and a warm, intimate atmosphere. Whisky is simply seductive.

More of the best in the North end

RESTAURANT
Boya
Boya, Oh Boya
3 Hata'arucha Street
Tel Aviv Port
Telephone (03) 5446166

RESTAURANT
Barbunia Bar
Fish and fries, with a secret side dish
192 Ben Yehuda Street
Telephone (03) 5240961

PIZZA
Beta pizza
The best pizza in town
Tel Aviv port
Delivery available
Telephone 1599509090

NIGHT LIFE
Shalvata
Saturday afternoon sunset at its best
Tel Aviv Port
Telephone (03) 5441279

NIGHT LIFE
Galina
Ocean breeze
Hangar 19, Tel Aviv Port
Telephone (03) 5445553

CAFE
Hurkanos
Neighborhood cafe
187 Ibn Gvirol Street
Telephone (03) 5467869

CAFE
Emily
Little cafe spot
30 Basel Street
Telephone (03) 5462714

CAFE
Elkalai
Gourmet coffee shop
1 Elkalai Street
Telephone (03) 6041260

CAFE
Moving
DVD cafe
308 Dizengoff Street
Telephone (03) 5444434

CAFE
Idelson 10
Anybody for an éclair?
252 Ben Yehuda Street
Telephone (03) 5444154

CAFE
Zorik
Coffee and friends
4 Yehuda Hamaccabi Street
Telephone (03) 6048858

FASHION
Kedem Sasson
Understanding fashion
213 Dizengoff Street
Telephone (03) 5232981

FASHION
Yossef
Oscar-night glam
213 Dizengoff Street
Telephone (03) 5298991

SPA
Villa Spa
When you need to be pampered
10 Yehuda Hamaccabi Street
Telephone (03) 5460608

City Center

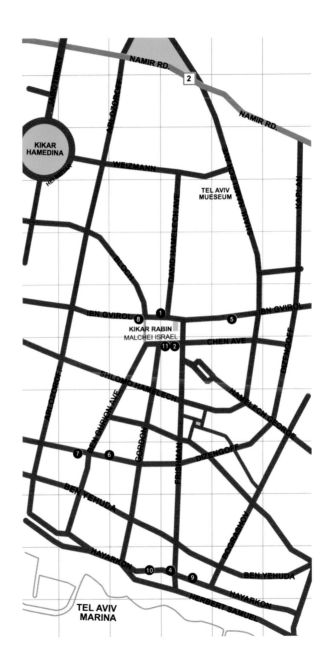

Welcome to the center of Tel Aviv. This is the bedrock of the city, home of the Tel Aviv Museum of Art, the New Israeli Opera and the main branch of the municipal library. It has lots of squares – Rabin Square, Dizengoff Square, Masaryk Square – although only one of them is actually square-shaped – plus three boulevards and a marina. Most of the residential sections are considered upscale, although this is more due to location than aesthetics. Some sections of central Tel Aviv were "uglified" during the 1970s. Dizengoff Square and Kikar Atarim are prime examples of what can kindly be called "errors in urban planning" – or less kindly, urban blight. Other parts were burnished during the 1980s and early 1990s, such as the eastern section of Shaul Hamelech (King Saul). And others still were left untouched – kept very much as they were in the 1940s, albeit very much in need of renovation. There are some very good shops in this area and many popular cafes. The very best restaurants tend to be clustered in the northern and southern sections of the city, but there are several good restaurants in this area that are worth a special trip. Central Tel Aviv is really the beating heart of the city. It may not be the most beautiful or historic section, although there are many examples of International style architecture on the side streets, but it is an excellent place to experience the city's unique rhythm and lifestyle. If you spend any significant time in Tel Aviv, you will probably end up visiting its center at least once.

Chen Boulevard, Ibn Gvirol and Rabin Square - Chen Boulevard is named after C.N. Bialik, Israel's poet laureate. The initial letters of his first two names form the Hebrew acronym Chen, which also means charm. It is an apt name for this quiet, residential boulevard, which begins at the Habimah Theater complex – home of Israel's national theater and the Israel Philharmonic Orchestra – and ends at Rabin Square. Few of the buildings are particularly attractive, but the street is shaded by heavy trees and lined with benches that are frequently occupied by the elderly, accompanied by their Philippine caregivers. A stroll down Chen Boulevard is a pleasant way to reach Rabin Square, Masaryk Square and the stretch of Ibn Gvirol that faces the municipal buildings and the Gan Ha'ir (City Garden) shopping complex. Masaryk Square is named for Thomas Masaryk, the first president of Czechoslovakia. Over the past few years several young designers have opened boutiques around here, selling their simple, youthful designs. There are also several good cafes, mostly overlooking the little square with the fountain in the middle. The significance of Rabin Square lies in its history and purpose, not in its design. Originally called Kings of Israel, the square was renamed after the late Prime Minister Yitzhak Rabin was assassinated on the square at a peace rally. A monument, including a diagram of Rabin's last movements, is beneath the steps of the municipality. Israelis gather at Rabin Square to celebrate, to mourn and to listen to live performances. It is a national monument of the best kind – a live one that is well used.Just behind the municipality building is the upscale Gan Ha'ir shopping center. When it first opened in the 1980s, Gan Ha'ir was considered the most elite upscale shopping center in the city. This is not the case anymore. There are still several elegant and expensive shops at Gan Ha'ir and it does cling to its elite image, but the atmosphere is an aging one. This is perhaps best illustrated by the Hungarian cafe, Yehudith's (Judith's), which feels like Mittel Europa with clusters of German-and-Hungarian-speaking elderly ladies consuming coffee with whipped cream and strudel. The food is mediocre at best and the service is grouchy, but Yehudith's aging clientele remains loyal nonetheless.The section of Ibn Gvirol facing the municipality is a hodgepodge of businesses ranging from popular, modern cafes and restaurants, falafel stands, fashionable boutiques and dim shops selling orthopedic shoes and support underwear that seem left over from another era. This is a busy place that is simultaneously a business district and a lively residential area. The area around Dubnov Street, which runs in a vaguely parallel line to Ibn Gvirol, is considered upscale – but mostly for its population rather than its architectural value. It was designed and built during the 1950s to woo the wealthy American Jews who never came; it has a garden city look, with generous plots of land and lots of green areas surrounding the residences, as well as a large park that is well maintained.

King Saul Boulevard (Shaul Hamelech) - Shaul Hamelech, as locals invariably call it, feels big and impersonal. It lacks the charm of the narrower, tree-lined boulevards and is far more traffic-clogged. But this is where the Tel Aviv Museum of Modern Art is located, as well as the new structure housing the New Israeli Opera, the main branch of the municipal public library and an art-house cinema. The Museum of Modern Art is not a particularly lovely building, but it has some very good permanent and temporary exhibitions. Many of Israel's most famous artists exhibit here. There are also exhibitions for children and live performances.

Central Dizengoff and Ben Gurion Boulevard - The central stretch of Dizengoff has a mix of cafes and shops that are pretty mainstream, with a few exceptions. This is a busy hub of activity, though, with plenty of strollers and people watching.The ugly round pedestrian bridge with the monstrous colored fountain in the middle is one of the primary examples of really ugly

1970s Tel Aviv architecture. Internationally renowned kinetic sculptor Yaacov Agam, who recently had a European retrospective, won a competition to design the fountain, which was supposed to symbolize fire and water. The municipality's intentions were good – they wanted to allow easier flow of traffic below the bridge while contributing to the city's cultural heritage. Unfortunately, there was never enough money to maintain the square with the fountain, and it has now become one of the biggest controversies in Tel Aviv. There is a plan to destroy and rebuild it, but no agreement on how the rebuilding should be handled; many want the original square, which was at ground level, to be restored – but that would create enormous traffic problems. The controversy is illustrative of the passion Tel Avivians feel for their city, as well as their conflicting visions. The bridge did kill off most of the commercial activity on this section of Dizengoff. Now it is a popular nighttime gathering place for teenage punk rockers, while during the day there are sometimes street performers. On Tuesdays there is a flea market under the bridge. If you're looking for 1970s LP of a long-forgotten pop singer, or a cut-glass candy dish that looks like the one your grandmother had, this is the place to shop. Ben Gurion Boulevard is also mostly residential and somewhat neglected looking. But it is popular with strollers and has some "interesting" modern sculptures by local artists on the stretch between Dizengoff and Kikar Atarim. Which brings us to the second example of horrible 1970s municipal planning. Kikar Atarim is the square overlooking the beach at the foot of Ben Gurion Boulevard – where, by the way, you can visit David Ben Gurion's home. Originally planned as a shopping mall, Atarim was left semi-complete and is a true eyesore. A few over-priced tourist restaurants serving greasy, semi-edible Israeli-style fast food and beers populate the square. The square's saving grace is the view of the beach and the marina. As with the Dizengoff pedestrian bridge, there are yet-to-be-realized plans to renovate Kikar Atarim – as soon as the funding is found and an agreement between the residents and the municipality reached. On Saturdays there is folk dancing on the pavement beneath the stairs that lead down to the beach – it's a nice local custom to check out.

Brasserie [1]

70 Ibn Gvirol Street
Telephone (03) 6967111

Sooner or later, everyone comes to the Brasserie, an homage to Art Deco, nicotine-stained walls and Parisian grand brasseries. Open 24 hours in the spirit of Brasserie Lip and La Copoule in Paris, the space has a decidedly Parisian aura and looks perfectly worn, down to the cigarette-stained tiled ceiling and worn floorboards. It is the hip younger sibling of a Tel Aviv landmark, the Coffee Bar. The Brasserie opened its doors four years ago and is credited with rejuvenating Ibn Gvirol, one of the city's main streets. They come for the star-studded clientele, the gay and jazzy atmosphere, the meticulous attention to hand-crafted Art Deco details and, of course, the food that never fails to please. The iconoclastic menu in French and Hebrew features winsomely prepared standards such as steak tartar, fresh oysters on the half shell, braised short ribs, Choucroute Garni, moules frites, pot au feu, Boeuf Bourguignon and coq au vin. The list goes on and on in the quest to satisfy the varied tastes of the Brasserie's clientele throughout the day and night.

Mayu [2]

7 Malchei Israel, Kikar Rabin
Telephone (03) 5273992
61 Ussishkin, Ramat Hasharon
Telephone (03) 5499033

Mayu, a small boutique with a warm and helpful staff located just opposite Rabin Square, personifies youthful Tel Aviv style. Designer/owner Maya Zukerman is a Tel Avivian, born and bred, who seems to have absorbed the city's Zeitgeist. She expresses it perfectly with her collections of casual, fashionable clothes that are sexy in an appealingly understated way. The garments are body conscious, but not too clingy or tight. The fabrics are almost all natural fibers that breathe, making them well suited to the long, hot and humid summers. In addition to her own designs, Zuckerman sells whimsical and sporty accessories such as belts, shoes and bags that complete the breezy, insouciant look favored by style-conscious Tel Aviv women in their twenties, thirties and forties. A new branch of Mayu recently opened in Ramat Hasharon, an upscale bedroom community just a few minutes' drive north of Tel Aviv.

FASHION

Gertrud [3]
225 Dizengoff Street
Telephone (03) 5467747

Gertrud has been around since 1991, which says a lot in this
city of fly-by-night fashion. This is the place to buy lovely,
oh-so-worth-the-cost, feminine clothes. The prevailing
theme is influenced by the lingerie look, whether it is a lace-
edged cotton camisole for daytime or a slinky, sexy evening
gown. In addition to Gertrud's original designs, you can find
contemporary European designer clothes – such as Day and
Suzanne Rutzou (Denmark) and Just In Case (Belgium).
Gertrud's collections are often featured in all the prominent
fashion magazines. For those who long for the Gertrud look
at a lower price, there is "Little Gertrud" on Masaryk Square.
There you can find the same excellent quality and winsome,
flirty look as at the older sister boutique.

Prima Tel Aviv [4]
105 Hayarkon Street
Telephone (03) 5206666

Prima Tel Aviv is a boutique hotel that combines style and intimacy in a beachfront location that is just steps from the center of the city. The interior was recently renovated in a minimalist, modern, relaxing style that is home-like and comfortable. During the evenings, candles are lit in the lobby area to maximize the living room effect, while chill out music plays in the background. Amenities include a chic bar area, a full range of business services, including conference rooms and wireless access, and a traditional Israeli breakfast that makes lunch a superfluous meal.

chameleon: snack-happy or hearty; savoury or sweet; thick and chewy in broth or thin and crispy in stir-fries. Try noodles.

Giraffe [5]
49 Ibn Gvirol Street
Telephone (03) 6916294

Giraffe is a trendy New York-style noodle bar that serves up generous portions of very fresh and tasty Asian fusion food. An open kitchen dominates the sleek white interior, so diners can watch as the chefs chop, dice and expertly toss the ingredients in large woks. The outdoor seating area is nearly always full, especially at mealtimes, no matter what the season. This is an excellent place for people watching, as Giraffe is popular with Tel Aviv's young, fashionable and beautiful. Standout dishes include sushi, tender chicken sate served with a savory peanut sauce, and a spicy Thai noodle soup richly flavored with coconut and studded with shrimp, calamari and vegetables.

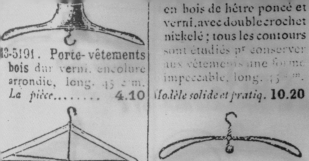

FASHION

Ronen Chen [6]

155 Dizengoff Street
Telephone (03) 5275672
49 Sheinkin Street
Telephone (03) 5280360

Ronen Chen is a popular Israeli designer who has also built his brand in the international arena. Chen's collections are particularly known for their clean lines, which are inspired by geometric shapes. He achieves his easy, comfortable, yet feminine look by draping fabrics on a mannequin, rather than sketching them on paper. With eight concept stores under the Ronen Chen name in Israel, the brand is also sold at 50 additional boutiques and specialty stores around the country. In addition, Ronen Chen's designs are sold throughout the world, predominantly in the U.S., Ireland, Canada and the Netherlands. The look is fashionable but not trendy, the fabrics are high quality, the workmanship is good and the prices are reasonable. Chen has hit on a winning formula that appeals to a wide variety of women, and for good reason.

Katomenta [7]
173 Dizengoff Street
Telephone (03) 5279899

Located in the heart of Tel Aviv's fashion district, Katomenta is a concept boutique that is more than just a place to buy clothes. One of Israel's most famous names in high fashion, Katomenta's reputation is based on designer Haya Nir's innovative, alternative approach to fashion. Her many admirers, who include some of Israel's best-known celebrities, have made the boutique into a cult-gathering place. Nir has twice been crowned Israeli Designer of the Year. Among the unique items in the store is a large range of thin muslin, silk and satin dresses and skirts, capturing the signature girly, lightly-lingerie look. The eclectic design, the retro furniture, books and strong mix of colors express the designer's personal touch. The high-end eveningwear line is located on the recently opened second floor. It is joined by the newly launched Maison Rouge collection for men, which targets the male counterpart to Katomenta's female clientele.

Tollman's [8]
Gan Ha'ir, 71 Ibn Gvirol Street
Telephone (03) 5223236

Tollman's is the place to shop for prestigious brand names in contemporary home accessories. This is the first stop for lovers of modern design. The upscale chain has exclusive import rights for mainly European designs, such as Alessi design accessories and Molteni, Cappellini and Cassina furniture. The flagship store in Gan Ha'ir (City Garden), Tel Aviv's luxury shopping complex, is pure eye candy. It is packed with merchandise, but does not feel at all crowded. The look and feel is airy, sleek and contemporary, making for a very pleasant shopping experience. The staff is knowledgeable and helpful.

HOTEL

Dan Tel Aviv [9]
99 Hayarkon Street
Telephone (03) 5202525
Reservations (03) 5202552

The Dan Tel Aviv is justifiably considered one of Tel Aviv's very best. Like most of the city's hotels – and all its luxury hotels – the Dan faces the beach and offers some pretty spectacular views from the rooms on the upper floors. The clean, modernist design of the lobby murmurs "luxury," as do the very well-appointed rooms. Nice touches include smart phones and luxury bath products. Services and amenities include a spa/gym complex and a wide range of shops selling high-end goods. The Philippe Starck-inspired bar is half a floor down from the lobby, creating an intimate atmosphere conducive to quiet conversation. The Dan Tel Aviv flagship restaurant - La Regence - offers a creative menu that combines the colorful, modern Israeli cuisine with the classic simplicity of the Mediterranean kitchen.

Sheraton Tel Aviv   [10]
115 Hayarkon Street
Telephone (03) 5211111

One of the Sheraton Tel Aviv & Towers' biggest draws is its prime location. Like most of the city's hotels it overlooks the beach, with well-furnished and spotlessly clean rooms that offer spectacular views up and down the coast – from Jaffa in the south to the Reading power terminal in the north. The hotel is also just steps from the shops and cafes on central Dizengoff Street, the art galleries on Gordon Street and some of the city's best nightlife. The Olive Leaf restaurant's chefs, Eyal Rosenberg and David Bitton, put to rest forever the myth that kosher food cannot be gourmet.

CAFE/BOOK SHOP

Tola'at Sefarim (Bookworm) [11]
9 Kikar Rabin Street
Telephone (03) 5298490

Tola'at Sefarim (Bookworm) is a very civilized Tel Aviv
institution that provides food for the mind and the body. It
combines the best of the city's cafe and intellectual life in a
relaxed, unpretentious environment. The bookshop specializes
in psychology, architecture and design, but also has a well-
chosen selection of prose, poetry, children's literature and
general non-fiction in both Hebrew and English. If you've just
stopped by on your own for a glass of wine, coffee and cake or
a light meal, the staff has stocked the cafe with a selection of
books to keep you company. If you like the book you happen
to have chosen, you can buy it on your way out.

More of the best in the City center

RESTAURANT
El Pastio
Fresh, fresh, fresh pasta
27 Ibn Gvirol Street
Telephone (03) 5251166

RESTAURANT
Lilit
Ideology on top
4 Dafna Street
Telephone (03) 6091331

RESTAURANT
Meat Bar
Reliable old-timer
52 Chen Boulevard
Telephone (03) 6956276

RESTAURANT
Raphael
Middle East meets West
87 Hayarkon Street
Telephone (03) 5226464

RESTAURANT
Toto
Fine Italian dining
4 Berkovich Street
Telephone (03) 6935151

CAFE
Lilush
Panini - Israeli style
73 Frishman Street
Telephone (03) 5379354

CAFE
Cafe Masaryk
Neighborhood institution
12 Masaryk Square
Telephone (03) 5272411

CAFE
Shine
Not Soho, but definitely cool
38 Shlomo Hamelech Street
Telephone (03) 5276186

CAFE
Lechem Erez
Upscale bread
52 Ibn Gvirol Street
Telephone (03) 6965680

CAFE
Meshulash
Survived the '90s with loyal clientele
168 Dizengoff Street
Telephone (03) 5236734

CAFE
Batcho
Coffee, ice cream, cakes
85 King George Street
Telephone (03) 5289753

CAFE
Libra
A good cafe on a street porch
120 Ben Yehuda Street
Telephone (03) 5298764

NIGHT LIFE
Fetish
The kinkiest place in Tel Aviv
48 King George Street

NIGHT LIFE
Molly Bloom's
The Irish are here!
2 Mendeli Sreet
Telephone (03) 5221558

FASHION
Dorin Frankfurt
The grand lady
164 Dizengoff Street
Telephone (03) 5270374

FASHION
Shufra shoes
Quality European impact
108 Dizengoff Street
Telephone (03) 5247274

FASHION
Doron Ashkenazi
The men's store for after your
first paycheck
187 Dizengoff Street
Telephone (03) 5272679

FASHION
Sarah Brown
Jessica Parker has left the
building
162 Dizengoff Street
Telephone (03) 5299902

FASHION
Ido Recanati
Sophisticated geometric design
13 Malchei Israel Street
Telephone (03) 5298481

HOTEL
Hilton Tel Aviv
Power lunch for MPs
Independence Garden
Telephone (03) 5202222

DVD &MUSIC
The Third Ear
Film student hangout
48 King George Street
Telephone (03) 6215201

tel aviv museum

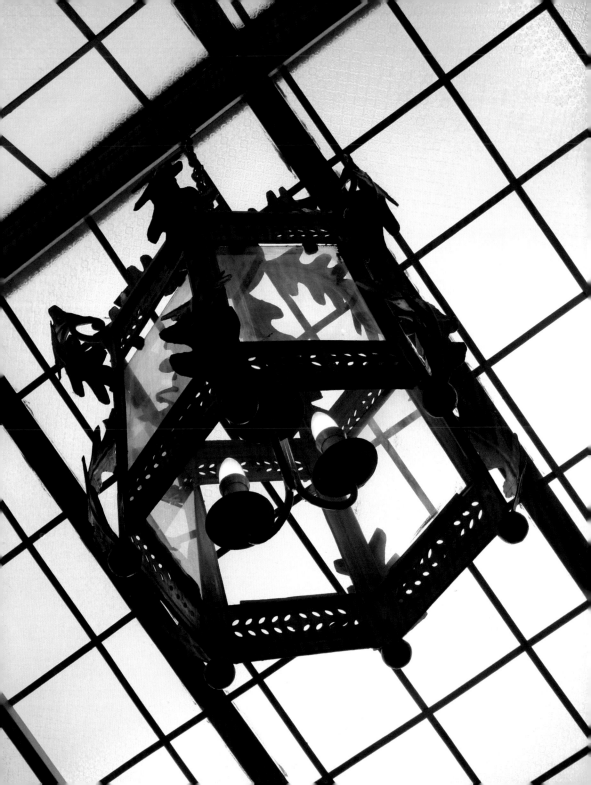

The heart
of Tel Aviv

The area of Tel Aviv that extends from Allenby Street to Dizengoff Center is one of the city's most vibrant. It is packed with things to do and see, from throbbing outdoor markets and "ethnic" neighborhoods to upscale boutiques and elegant dining.

Allenby Street - Given its very run-down look, it's difficult to believe Allenby was once Tel Aviv's most elegant street – its "grand boulevard." That was in the days of the British Mandate, from the 1920s to the late 1940s. Back then Allenby, from Rothschild to King George Street, was the city's hub, its commercial center, known for its furriers, bookbinders, cafes and boutiques. Today one's first impression of Allenby is noisy, exhaust-spewing diesel buses, falafel stands, shops selling cheap goods imported from the developing world and moneychangers. But look carefully behind the tree tops and you will see some beautiful, though sadly neglected, old buildings from the 1920s. Some have a sign in mosaic tiles telling the date on which it was built and the names of the architect and owner. Lately, there are signs that Allenby may be on the cusp of a renaissance. There are a couple of good restaurants tucked away behind discreet signs and set back from the street; there are also a few interesting bars and some very good second-hand bookshops.

Ahad Ha'am Street - Named after Asher Ginzburg, whose pen name was Ahad Ha'am (One Nation), this is one of Tel Aviv's longest streets. It is also one of the most architecturally eclectic and historically interesting. The foot of Ahad Ha'am is in Neve Tzedek, where Shabazi Street ends. The boxy white Shalom Tower was once the site of the Gymnasia Herzliya, which was originally founded in 1905 as the first high school where all the subjects were taught in modern Hebrew. Some of Israel's most famous literary figures, like the poet Avraham Shlonsky and the writer Aharon Meged, studied at the Gymnasia Herzliya. Past Allenby, the buildings lining Ahad Ha'am are very eclectic. There is the tall 1980s-style office tower that houses the stock exchange, eclectic old 1920s buildings that are in a terrible state of disrepair and many examples of 1930s International style apartment buildings – some renovated, others not.

Montefiore and Melchett Square - Montefiore is parallel to Ahad Ha'am. A nice way to enter the street is to turn left from Ahad Ha'am on Karl Netter, a short, leafy side street opposite the stock exchange. Then turn right at Montefiore, walk up two minutes and you will arrive at Melchett Square, also called Albert Square – after one of King George V's sons. This is one of the most magical squares in Tel Aviv. The striking Pagoda House dominates the square, which connects Melchett, Nachmani and Montefiore streets. Originally built as a hotel, the Pagoda House was abandoned for years; about six years ago it was completely renovated and is now occupied by a private family. But while the Pagoda House is the most arresting structure overlooking the square, each of the streets that converge here has a building in a unique architectural style – ranging from Levantine to eclectic to International. This is a fascinating place to examine the brief, rich history of Tel Aviv – as told by its architecture. The best place to sit and enjoy this little story about Tel Aviv is from the vantage point of the bench, shaded by an enormous old tree, on the little traffic island in the middle of the square.

The Carmel Market - The Carmel Market is the largest outdoor market in Tel Aviv. Its narrow, twisting streets are lined with stalls and shops selling everything from toiletries and clothes to meat and produce, all at rock-bottom prices. Despite the presence of several Russian delicatessens, the overwhelming majority of the shops and stands are owned by Israelis of North African descent, giving the market a distinctly "Mizrachi" (Eastern) flavor. The shoppers, however, come from all over the world. This is the place to experience Israel's modern melting pot. The people who shop here include native-born Israelis, new immigrants and foreign workers from all over the globe – from China to Ghana. Many of the shops carry goods that cater to foreign workers, like fufu flakes, soya sauce and tofu. The best time to visit is midday on Friday, when the merchants of perishable goods lower their prices with loud shouts and the foreign workers, just released from work, come to buy food for the coming weekend. The pirated compact disc merchants pump up the volume on their stereos, and the atmosphere becomes positively frenetic.

The Nachalat Binyamin Pedestrian Mall - Nachalat Binyamin is actually a very long street that extends deep into the Florentine neighborhood, but the section that parallels the Carmel Market starting at Gruzenberg Street and curving up toward Allenby, opposite Sheinkin Street, is closed to vehicular traffic. This pedestrian mall is lined with a variety of shops that specialize mostly in fabric, inexpensive furniture and a hodgepodge of "ethnic" clothes imported from India. There are also a few cafes and a couple of popular restaurants in the area. But the main reason to visit Nachalat Binyamin is the outdoor craft market on Tuesdays and Fridays, when it resembles market day in a medieval European city –with a Middle Eastern twist. On these days there are endless tables displaying an amazing variety of arts and crafts that range from straight kitsch to beautiful kitsch. There are candles, pottery, glass blowers, hand-made puppets, lamps – the list is endless. Fridays on Rashi Street, there are live street performances by amateur musicians, acrobats and jugglers. Black Hebrews from Dimona – African-Americans who believe they are the original Jews – braid and bead hair for a fee and Peruvian musicians play traditional wind instruments and guitars to accompany themselves as they sing songs in Spanish. There is also a very popular food stall staffed by a Druze family that sells enormous homemade flatbreads baked on the spot by a traditional method. Just follow your nose – you can't miss it.

The Yemenite Vineyard/Kerem Hateymanim - It's tempting to use words like "quaint" and "charming" to describe this tiny neighborhood just beyond the Carmel Market. Originally founded in the 1930s by immigrants from Yemen (hence its name), the area gradually fell into decline in the decades following the establishment of the state. About 12 years ago the municipality made some serious investments in the infrastructure; since then the winding streets have gradually been "discovered" by bohemian Tel Avivians looking for inexpensive housing, and many of the old buildings have been nicely renovated. But despite the influx of the artsy crowd, the area is still heavily populated by old-timers and hasn't lost its authenticity. If you're in the mood for some spicy Yemenite food in a no-frills environment, there are plenty of little restaurants to try.

Rothschild Boulevard - Rothschild is easily the loveliest boulevard in Tel Aviv. Hundreds of people stroll and cycle along its tree-shaded paths every day. Its benches are a popular gathering place for people of all ages, and at night there are often spontaneous neighbourhood games of petanques on the gravel-filled rectangles set aside for that purpose. The buildings that line Rothschild are very eclectic – from that odd hodgepodge Levantine/European/Ottoman style of the 1920s, to International, to modern office towers.

Gan Hachashmal - Gan Hachashmal (The Electricity Garden) was so named because it was once the site of Tel Aviv's main electricity plant. Until about two years ago it was primarily known as an extremely seedy area of peepshows, underage male prostitutes and junkies – even though it is only 100 meters from Rothschild Boulevard. Many of the apartments in the area are gorgeous examples of classic Bauhaus design, but for years the landlords could find tenants only if they were willing to accept a symbolic rent. Few people ventured into Gan Hachashmal at night and even fewer were brave enough to live there. Now it is one of the most up-and-coming areas of Tel Aviv, with a nice mix of commercial and residential buildings surrounding the completely renovated square. This might end up being the equivalent of New York's SoHo neighborhood.

Sheinkin Street - Following a decline that began in the 1950s, when many residents moved to northern Tel Aviv, Sheinkin was "discovered" by the cafe crowd in the early 1980s and became the heart of Israel's artist-bohemian scene for the next two decades. Sheinkin was, and to many still is, the place for actors, musicians, writers, and all those who like to be associated with them, to see and be seen. The street's name is also sometimes used to express derision: "Sheinkin types," pronounced with a sneer in one's voice, means "artsy fartsy bleeding heart leftists." Lately Sheinkin has lots its edge a bit, but it is still one of the most popular and well-known streets in Tel Aviv – and possibly in Israel. Among the fascinating anomalies of life in the Sheinkin area is the very visible presence of a large Hasidic community. Modestly dressed, bewigged women and men in traditional black coats live quietly and in apparent harmony alongside the scantily clad, tattooed and pierced. This is a striking contrast with Jerusalem, where the secular and religious frequently clash over communal and lifestyle issues. The northern end of Sheinkin between Rothschild and the little square that ends at Yochanan Hasandlar is more sedate: Here you will find the more upscale boutiques, cafes and restaurants. After the park and continuing down to Allenby, the street becomes a tad seedy. Most of the shops on this end sell cheap designer apparel knock offs meant for teenagers, and the cafes are nothing special. On Friday, the first day of the weekend, the street is packed with teenagers from all over the greater Tel Aviv area. On that day the locals avoid Sheinkin.

Bograshov Street - Bograshov Street starts at Hayarkon Street and ends at King George, which is also one of Tel Aviv's longest and most important streets. Bograshov is not a particularly interesting thoroughfare, although there are some nice examples of Bauhaus apartment buildings on the side streets, particularly Shalom Aleichem and Tchernichovsky.

Bialik Street and the old cemetery - If you do detour off Bograshov Street, the old cemetery between Pinsker and Chovevei Zion (Lovers of Zion) is the resting place of some of Israel's most famous literary figures. Chaim Nachman Bialik, Israel's poet laureate, is buried there, as is Saul Tchernichovsky and many other famous names in Hebrew literature. This is Tel Aviv's equivalent of the Pere Lachaise cemetery in Paris. From there it is very worthwhile to veer off to Bialik Street, which is a lovely cul de sac dominated by the poet's original home, now a museum. The famous Israeli artist Reuven Rubin also lived on Bialik and his home, too, is a museum in which many of his iconic paintings are exhibited and his life chronicled.

Meir Park - Turn right at King George, walk for a couple of minutes and you'll arrive at Gan Meir, or Meir Park – named for Meir Dizengoff, the first mayor of Tel Aviv. The circular oasis of bench-lined, tree-shaded paths, a fishpond and a playground was recently refurbished and is now a popular place to hang out. The city noise fades as soon as you enter through the main gates; suddenly, you can hear birds chirping. Meir Park also has the largest and most popular dog run in the city.

Dizengoff Center - Dizengoff Center, Israel's first shopping mall, was built in the 1970s at the corner of King George and Dizengoff. It has long been surpassed in elegance and variety by the newer shopping malls in Tel Aviv's northern suburbs, but it's a popular and convenient place to shop for a wide, if standard, selection of clothes, household goods and groceries. Dizengoff Center is a classic example of Israeli 1970s "ugly architecture," but it has a nice, comfortable vibe that feels very communal – much more like an outdoor shopping area than a sterile, enclosed mall. There are branches of almost all the popular fast food restaurants, including Israel's homegrown coffee chains, plus two multiplex cinemas. The Lev cinema on the uppermost floor is more of an art-house cinema, whilst the cinema on the lowest floor screens current Hollywood releases. On Fridays there is a popular international food fair at Dizengoff Center. The corridors of the mall are lined with an astonishing variety of cooked food, from Moroccan to Chinese.

Kyoto Tel Aviv [1]

31 Montefiore Street
Telephone (03) 5661234

Kyoto is a stylish, chic restaurant with a menu that combines traditional Japanese cuisine with elements from the South American kitchen to create the ultimate fusion food – colorful, unique and delicious. The industrial-style decor is rescued from coldness by the colorfully painted walls and the enormous rectangular bar constructed of warm dark wood, as well as the carefully stacked layers of fish and seafood visible through the protective glass cases. A team of sushi chefs provide ongoing live theater as they expertly slice, dice and roll for the viewing pleasure of patrons perched on stools around the bar. The faultless food is prepared with great attention to aesthetic presentation and freshness; it also reflects the harmony with nature that is such a predominant theme in traditional Japanese cuisine. After dark, Kyoto is a romantic place to enjoy cocktails followed by an imaginative, palate-pleasing meal in that stylish atmosphere that is so representative of Tel Aviv. There is also a popular branch of Kyoto in Herzliya, with extensive outdoor seating.

RESTAURANT
Pronto [2]
26 Nachmani Street
Telephone (03) 5660915

Established in 1989, Pronto still sets the gold standard for Italian restaurants in Israel. Owner Rafi Adar, who lived for nearly a decade in Rome, was awarded the Order of Knighthood (Cavaliere della Repubblica Italiana) for his contribution to promoting Italian culture abroad; the framed certificate is displayed, proudly but without fanfare, near the bar. Like the decor, the food is simple, elegant and informal. The uncomplicated menu offers familiar Italian fare that starts with antipasti and salads and continues with pastas, risotto, meats and fish. There is an impressively wide selection of mostly Italian wines. Pronto is popular at lunchtime, particularly with well-heeled business people who are entertaining foreign visitors, and is booked solid each night for dinner as well. There is reserved parking for evening diners.

Helena [3]

4-a Tarsat Avenue, Jacob's Garden, Mann Auditorium
Telephone (03) 5289289

Located in the Habima cultural complex near Dizengoff Street, Helena is an attractive and popular 24-hour spot that has several personalities. During the day it is packed with businesspeople and politicians who appreciate its reliably good upscale cafe food, central location and convenient parking. Then there is the pre-theatre dinner crowd, from 6 to 8 P.M., followed by the late diners. At night Helena becomes a very happening lounge bar scene for the beautiful and the famous. But this is not an exclusive scene. The music is low-key groove, not heavy house or trance, and the staff is equally welcoming to regulars and first-timers. Around dawn Helena draws an eclectic crowd of clubbers ending a long night out, newspaper staff just off the graveyard shift and early risers out for breakfast.

RESTAURANT
Orna and Ella [4]
33 Sheinkin Street
Telephone (03) 6204753

Orna and Ella is one of Tel Aviv's great culinary institutions. It is an icon so famous that it has entered the national lexicon of cultural references – most especially for the legendary sweet potato pancakes. For many, this 12-year-old cafe and restaurant is the only truly important reason to visit Sheinkin Street. The two women behind the legend are, of course, Orna and Ella. Together they nurtured what began as a tiny cafe into a restaurant that serves a varied menu of mostly Italian and French-influenced dishes – such as salade Nicoise, pastas and famous desserts like tarte tatin. There are also daily specials that change according to the season. Everything, including the bread, is lovingly prepared on the premises from the finest and freshest ingredients. Many of the serving staff have worked there for years and they are invariably professional – not to mention famously good looking.

RESTAURANT
Cantina [5]
71 Rothschild Boulevard
Telephone (03) 6205051

The owners of Cantina aspire to an admirably simple goal: to serve good food prepared from the best and freshest ingredients for reasonable prices in a pleasant atmosphere. They succeed on all counts. Cantina is a comfortable, intimate restaurant that is devoid of pretense or gimmicks. The simple, pleasing decor features a heavy wood wrap-around bar, unadorned cream-colored walls and – perhaps most importantly – an attractive, friendly and efficient serving staff. The menu consists of standard southern Italian dishes such as pizzas, pastas and minestrone soup, as well as a wide selection of seafood, meat and fish dishes that are reliably fresh and well prepared. Some of the dishes have been tailored to suit the Israeli palate, meaning that the spice factor has been kicked up a notch or two. The outdoor seating area faces a particularly green and pleasant stretch of Rothschild Boulevard. Unsurprisingly, there is rarely an empty table at Cantina.

RESTAURANT
Cafe Noir [6]
43 Ahad Ha'am Street
Telephone (03) 5663018

Cafe Noir has been around for a decade, but is as popular today as it was when it first opened - at a time when there were few good restaurants in the area. The secret to its success is simple comfortable, old-fashioned decor, good service, a casual atmosphere and reliably good upscale comfort food. Cafe Noir's signature dish is its schnitzel, which is widely considered the best in Israel. Pounded thin, breaded and crisply fried in classic Viennese style, it can be ordered in chicken, veal or pork variety and is served with irresistible crispy fried potatoes. Like the food, the decor is very homey. The owner's own paintings hang on the walls, antique lamps provide a flattering, warm light and the dark wood tables look and feel very solid. Cafe Noir has many regulars, from the breakfast crowd of journalists and politicians to businesspeople who come for lunch through the locals who show up for dinner.

Armadillo [7]
51 Ahad Ha'am Street
Telephone (03) 6205573

Located just two minutes' walk from Sheinkin and Rothschild streets in the heart of Tel Aviv, Armadillo is the best kind of neighborhood bar. It's small, it's cozy, it's got style and yes – once you've been there a few times, chances are that everyone will know your name. This is a place to chill out over beers and homemade food at one of the tables, or to sit at the long bar and make some new friends. The music is always excellent, but the volume is never so loud that it overwhelms conversation.

Kisim [8]
8 Hachashmal Street
Telephone (03) 5604890

Designer Yael Rosen-Ben Shachar has a reputation for creating unique, high quality bags and wallets with clean, elegant lines. Each piece is carefully designed with a signature attention to detail that make Kisim bags instantly recognizable. A few years ago, she teamed up with designer Orly Cohen Alloro. Their collections of backpacks, daytime purses and evening bags are sold in Paris, Amsterdam, the United States and Canada – in addition to Israel. Recently, Yael opened a small shop in the Gan Hachashmal area, a rapidly developing center of hip, contemporary style, where she showcases her latest designs.

FASHION
Frau Blau [9]
8 Hachashmal Street
Telephone (03) 5601735

Fashion designer Helena Blaunstein and her partner, illustrator Philip Blau created Frau Blau designs as an expression of their humorous outlook on life and fashion. The name of the boutique is taken from the German slang for "drunken woman," and the keyhole design logo symbolizes the idea of a look into the designers' mad, magical and happy world. A surrealistic dialogue in Lewis Carroll's "Through the Looking Glass" inspires the 2006 collection, Tiger Lilies: Alice expresses the wish that the flowers could talk and they respond that they do – when they have something important to say.

FASHION
Delicatessen Clothing Boutique [10]
4 Barzilai Street
Telephone (03) 5602297

Designer Idit Barak's Delicatessen Boutique is only two years old, but it has already earned international acclaim in publications such as Metropolis, the Herald Tribune and Time Out. Barak and accessory designer Sharon Gurel chose the boutique's name because it evokes the notion of delicacy. Indeed, Barak's designs maintain a delicate – and successful – balance between practicality and concept. The look is playful, individual and sophisticated. The boutique's design, created by New York-based architect Guy Zucker, is constructed of unique materials, linoleum and cardboard tubes, that follow the logic of seasonal change in fashion.

CAFE/DESIGN

Gavriel [11]
42 Montefiore Street
Telephone (03) 5667020

Gavriel combines the eating and shopping experience and takes both to a whole new level. The eclectic decor of the hip, fashionable and cool restaurant features a potpourri of antiques and various objects found all over the world – from India to South America. The result is warm, pleasing and even romantic. The enclosed courtyard out back takes the romance factor and kicks it up a notch, with chairs upholstered in old-fashioned rose-patterned fabric and wooden tables painted white. The restaurant has been open for only a few months, but has already won wide critical praise for its food and is regularly listed as one of the 10 best casual restaurants in the country. The shop behind the cafe has a wide selection of beautiful home accessories, from Italian designer dishes to Crabtree & Evelyn toiletries, unique jewelry designs and many more difficult-to-find objects.

More of the best in the Heart

RESTAURANT
Pastis
Bistro on the boulevard
73 Rothschild Boulevard
Telephone (03) 5250773

RESTAURANT
The Thai House
Tel Aviv meets authentic Bangkok
8 Bograshov Street
Telephone (03) 5178568

RESTAURANT
Dita
Mother of all time crawlers
45 Rothschild Boulevard
Telephone (03) 5604222

RESTAURANT
Moses
Location, location, location
35 Rothschild Boulevard
Telephone (03) 5664949

RESTAURANT
Stephan Brown
All-time favorite
99 Allenby Street
Telephone (03) 5604725

NIGHT LIFE
Shoshana Johnson
Cool sister of all-time favorite
97 Allenby Street
Telephone (03) 5607443

CAFE
Ginzburg
Neighborhood cafe
55 Ahad Ha'am Street
Telephone (03) 5608070

CAFE
Cafe Noach
Sunday jazz at the secret
neighborhood hangout
93 Ahad Ha'am Street
Telephone (03) 6293799

CAFE
Cafe Tamar
Bohemian rhapsody on a Friday
morning
57 Sheinkin Street
Telephone (03) 6852376

CAFE
Loveat
A diner-concept cafe
1 Barzilai Street
Telephone (03) 5666696

CAFE
Cafe Bialik
Neighborhood cafe with a twist
2 Bialik Street
Telephone (03) 6200832

FASHION
Alma
Local hip
9 Ba'alei Melacha Street
Telephone (03) 6200145

FASHION
Dina Glass
Fashion gem
35 Nachmani Street
Telephone (03) 5602493

FASHION
Naama Bezalel
Jane Austin hip
40 Sheinkin Street
Telephone (03) 6293938

FASHION
Shani Bar
Shoes and bags designer
3 Mikve Israel Street
Telephone (03) 5605981

FASHION
Nait
Young fashion designer
10 Mikve Israel Street
Telephone (03) 5600402

DESIGN
Carrousel
Silver-spoon babies
27 Rothschild Boulevard
Telephone (03) 5603750

BOOK SHOP
Polak
Antique books
36 King George Street
Telephone (03) 5288613

South end

N

SHENKIN

YEHUDA HALEVI

HACHASHMAL

WOLFSON

SALAME

ROTHSCHILD Ave.

MONTIFIORE

EYAD HA'AM

ALLENBY

HA'ALIA

ALLENBY

NACHALAT BINYAMIN

YAFO Rd.

LEVINSKY

1

5

FLORENTIN

10
12

19

LILIENBLUM

HERTZEL

18

FLORENTIN

FRANKEL

HATAVOR

17

RAMBAM

2

VITAL

KEREM
HATEMANIM

3
7 4

6

ABARBANEL

11 NEVE TZEDEK

15

CHELOUCHE

8

SHABAZI

16

ELIFELET

9

HAYARKON

SALAME

ELIAT

PORIYYA

14

KAUFMAN

TIRCHA

13

JERUSALEM Blvd.

300m

Tel Aviv's oldest neighborhoods are in many ways the city's most vibrant. This is where some of the most fashionable clubs, boutiques and restaurants are concentrated, as well as some of the most interesting architecture. The area alternates between down-at-the-heels and chic bohemian, with struggling artists, musicians, actors and students making up the latter. There's a lot to see and experience in Old Tel Aviv. It would be very easy to spend several days slowly exploring, spending ample time in the cafes to soak up the vibrant atmosphere.

Neve Tzedek - Neve Tzedek (Oasis of Justice) is the city's oldest neighborhood and also its most picturesque, with an atmosphere that evokes an artists' colony or a little village. Twenty years ago it was practically a slum, as evidenced by photographs from the time that show rubble-filled empty lots and houses with collapsing roofs. Then the struggling artists discovered it, followed by the people with money who like to live among struggling artists. Now it is considered one of the most desirable addresses in Tel Aviv. Neve Tzedek was conceived and built in the 1880s, nearly three decades before Tel Aviv was founded in 1909. The Chelouche family, prominent Jewish residents of Jaffa, purchased and developed the property in order to create healthier, less crowded living conditions for the Jewish community of Jaffa. The houses bear no hint of Ottoman influence, but the large, square, two- and three-story homes don't seem European either. Some say the style is reminiscent of certain areas in Beirut. The Chelouche (pronounced and misspelled on the eponymous street as "Shlush") family home in Neve Tzedek is now a museum. The winding streets are lined with elegantly renovated late-19th century homes, fashionable cafes, bars and chic boutiques. Shabazi Street, in particular, is an excellent place to part with one's money in exchange for all sorts of beautiful things, from clothes to jewelry to unique crafts, or to linger over a good cappuccino at one of the outdoor cafes. The lovely Suzanne Dellal Center, home of the Batsheva Modern Dance Troupe, attracts culture vultures from all over the city – not to mention bridal parties who come to be photographed in the courtyard on Thursday afternoons, the most popular day to marry in Israel. And yet, despite all this gentrification, Neve Tzedek does not feel like a sterile yuppified neighborhood. It has charm and authenticity, and it feels comfortable, relaxed and unpretentious. There are reminders of the neighborhood's recent past. In between the expensively restored houses and the designer boutiques there is the occasional weed-and-litter-choked empty lot, sometimes decorated with the rusted hulks of abandoned cars. There are also old, unrenovated homes that are still inhabited by Yemenite families who moved into the area in the 1950s. Stroll around on a quiet Saturday morning, and you're sure to hear traditional chanting emerging from the open windows of the old synagogues.

The beach area: Dolphinarium Beach and Banana Beach - The strip of beach that borders Neve Tzedek is called Banana Beach. Despite the pervasive smell of urine and rotting garbage in the parking lot, Banana Beach is a popular hangout. It's also known as Drummer's Beach, for the amateur drummers who gather there on Friday afternoons at sunset for a "welcome to the weekend" session. Anyone can participate in the drumming, which continues until late at night and attracts jugglers, dancers and capoeira enthusiasts – as well as dozens of people who just come to enjoy the quintessentially laid back Tel Aviv atmosphere.Directly across the street is Hassan Bek, the only functioning mosque on the Tel Aviv side of Tel Aviv-Jaffa. The muezzin juts up against the background of modern high-rise hotels, providing an oft-photographed contrast between old and new.Just to the south, Charles Clore Park is a popular place to picnic – especially on Saturday afternoons, when dozens of families grill meat on portable barbecues and spit piles of empty sunflower seeds onto the grass. The spot is particularly popular with Arabs from nearby Jaffa and foreign workers from the Philippines.

Lilienblum Street - Technically part of Neve Tzedek, Lilienblum is a side street that connects Allenby Street to Neve Tzedek's Pines (unfortunately pronounced "penis") Street. For years, until the 1970s, it was Israel's Wall Street. The Bank of Israel was headquartered on Lilienblum, as were the moneychangers who circumvented the country's then strict foreign currency trading laws. After the stock exchange moved up to Ehad Ha'am and later in the decade foreign currency regulations were lifted, Lilienblum lost its luster and became shabby and dull with nothing to distinguish it but a few neglected buildings and dusty shops. But over the past decade it was rediscovered and has rapidly become one of the main hubs of Tel Aviv's nightlife. Today the street is lined with very hip lounge bars and restaurants-cum-bars that usually hit their peak after midnight, making it one of the best places to experience Tel Aviv's famous nightlife. Don't even bother trying to find a parking space in the vicinity between 11 p.m. and 3 a.m. on a weekend night. It's an exercise in futility.

Nachalat Binyamin - The section of Nachalat Binyamin that stretches from Gruzenberg Street to Ahad Ha'am is full of stylish bars and some top restaurants. Like Lilienblum, this part of Nachalat Binyamin has a happening nightlife scene.

Florentine - Florentine is an interesting combination of fashionable cool (although a little raw around the edges) and solid, ethnic working class. In the early 1990s it seemed to be on the cusp of a major renewal. It was then that Eitan Fucks, the director of the hit Israeli movie "Walk on Water," produced a television series that was named after the neighborhood and featured a group of twentysomething polyamorous artists and musicians living a cool, urban existence. The show became a cult hit, and many thought the neighborhood was going to be the next Tel Aviv success story. But Florentine has quite a few drawbacks: The infrastructure is not in the best condition, and there is a lot of street noise and pollution from the local industry. The expected renaissance did not happen, and during the late 1990s landlords were hard-pressed to find tenants for their newly renovated apartments. The situation worsened after 2000, when the global economic downturn and the suicide bombers hit Tel Aviv hard. Rents in the more desirable neighborhoods went down, students moved in with their parents to save money, and Florentine was left to the veteran residents and foreign workers. Recently, though, Florentine seems to be going through yet another tentative renewal – in tandem with Israel's rapidly improving economy. The renovated apartments are finding eager tenants – people who have been pushed out of other neighborhoods by rising rents. There are trendy bars, restaurants and cafes along Florentine Street and several of the side streets, as well as some very popular nightclubs. In some parts of Florentine, 2 a.m. feels like the middle of the afternoon. Other parts of Florentine remain traditional. The colorful food market on Levinsky Street is well worth checking out. Here you can find everything from exotic spices and dried fruit to freshly baked Turkish flatbread and cheese-filled savory pastries. Most of the merchants are Jews from the mediterranean basin, and many speak to one another in Ladino, or Judaeo-Spanish. Many of Florentine's streets are devoted to a single product – such as bedroom furniture, kitchen accessories, cheap clothing and lighting fixtures. There are also streets devoted to a single craft, like carpentry or upholstering. The local merchants have known each other for decades, with many passing on the business from one generation to the next. As a result, there is a unique culture based on shared experience, history – and even, in some cases, terminology. Everything here is custom made, with many of the country's most famous furniture and accessories designers located here. For those who care about unique style and abhor commercialism, Florentine is the first – and often only – destination. Sadly, the traditional Florentine culture is on the cusp of dying out. The family businesses are in the third generation; many offspring have decided to branch out into their own professions and the municipality is trying to push out the wholesale merchants because of overcrowding. So far the merchants have successfully opposed this move but in the end the municipality will probably win. Now is really the time to visit Florentine in order to witness the last years of a thriving, colorful and traditional lifestyle.

The Old Central Bus Station - If you want to see Tel Aviv's gritty inner city, this is the place to go. The Old Central Bus Station area is known mainly for shops that sell pirated CDs, knockoff designer jeans and secondhand electronic goods and furniture. Most of the residents are foreign workers or new immigrants, and there are lots of food shops that cater specifically to their tastes – like pork butchers with signs in Chinese and Russian. On Friday afternoons, as the weekend begins, many of the foreign workers gather at cheap outdoor pubs on the Neve Sha'anan pedestrian mall to relax with a beer after a long week of manual labor. If you're an urban anthropologist this could be an interesting stop. Otherwise, there's not much to see.

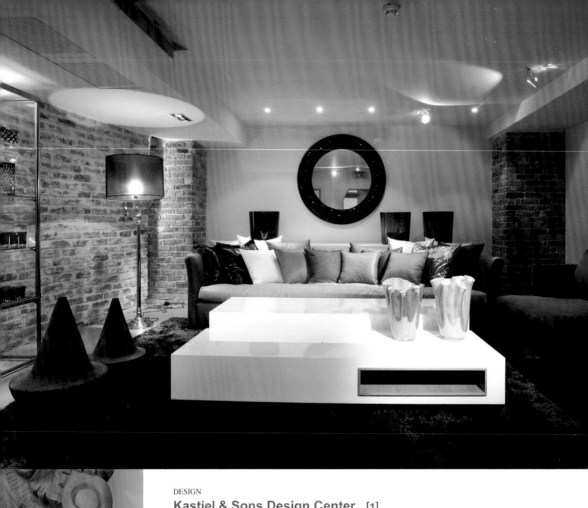

DESIGN

Kastiel & Sons Design Center [1]
9 Wolfson Street
Telephone (03) 6836334

Kastiel is one of the most prestigious names in furniture and interior design in Israel – and also among the international jet set. The six-level Florentine showroom is at the original location in which it was established by Efraim Kastiel 60 years ago, and then handed down to his sons. In addition to the furniture, which they still manufacture at their own factory just down the street, the Kastiel showroom is packed with unique accessories, rugs and sculptures. The paintings on the walls are original works, and are also for sale. This is not merely a place to buy beautiful, custom-designed furniture for your home; the Kastiel brothers provide full interior design services, customizing the look of the home to match the customer's needs and desires. If they do not manufacture a necessary item, they will obtain it for you. They also export their furniture to private customers around the world. The September 2006 Architectural Digest features a photographic essay on Yehoshua and Anat Kastiel's North Tel Aviv home. The photos illustrate a vision that is quite striking and unique: it is contemporary yet timeless, elegant and comfortable. The Kastiels do not advertise; word of mouth does the job just fine, thank you very much. Efraim's sons are happy to tell you that they have designed furniture for all of Israel's presidents and nearly all its prime ministers. They might mention in passing that their international clients send private jets to transport them. But then they will emphasize strongly that they give equal consideration to customers who wish to purchase a single item.

RESTAURANT

Carmella Bistro   [2]
14 Rambam Street
Telephone (03) 5161417

Carmella Bistro is housed in a beautifully restored old building on the outskirts of the Nachalat Binyamin quarter, just steps away from the Carmel Market from which it derives its name. Nostalgia and warmth fairly seep out of the mosaic floors, small terraces and intimate, high-ceilinged rooms. Carmela is truly a uniquely Tel Aviv dining experience. Chef Daniel Zach chose the location for its proximity to the market, which he visits daily for inspiration and the freshest possible ingredients. The Mediterranean-style cuisine includes seafood, the best meats available and seductive homemade bread. For those who want a taste of it all without sampling from fellow diners' plates, Zach has come up with a very appealing tasting experience. All the dishes listed on the main menu can be ordered in smaller portions and served in a manner designed for group dining. It is possible to order half portions to increase the variety. Carmella is justifiably praised for offering the most comprehensive list of Israeli wines in the country, including boutique wineries and limited edition vintages. The bistro offers a constantly changing selection of three of Zach's most recent discoveries, elegantly served in 250 ml carafes on a custom-made tray. A sommelier is available to help choose the wine best suited to the food.

Samy D. [3]
56 Shabazi Street
Telephone (03) 5164968

Samy D. fuses art and function with his stunning ceramic dishes. His use of deep, eye-catching color and his delicate designs have revolutionized the world of ceramics both in Israel and abroad, where they are sold at some of the most exclusive shops in the world. In addition to the dishes on display in his Neve Tzedek shop, Samy D. designs custom-made items for international art galleries and museums. Art critics are hard-pressed to find enough superlatives for his designs and his use of color. Samy D. has developed a special kiln process that makes these dishes both beautiful and strong.

Orit Ivshin [4]
53 Shabazi Street
Telephone (03) 5160811

The jewelry Orit Ivshin crafts and sells in her studio in Neve Tzedek is well suited to the neighborhood. Like Neve Tzedek, Ivshin's pieces look simultaneously modern and influenced by the past. Ivshin uses gold, silver and semi-precious stones to craft simple, attractive pieces with pleasingly clean lines. They seem to suit nearly everyone, no matter how the wearer defines her personal style. Because they are neither bulky nor overly delicate, Orit Ivshin jewelry is the kind one wears constantly. It takes on the wearer's personality and becomes part of her "look."

Arik Ben Simhon [5]
110 Nachalat Binyamin
Telephone (03) 6837865

Arik Ben Simhon is one of the biggest names in the Israeli design scene. Chances are that if you have spent time in a trendy Tel Aviv bar, restaurant or club, you have sat on a Ben Simhon couch or dined at a Ben Simhon table. The Ben Simhon look is unmistakably modern, but it is also timeless. It is a pleasure to spend time browsing in his large South Tel Aviv showroom, soaking up the atmosphere of luxury and comfort.

Slide into a deep, wide Ben Simhon couch, stroke the buttery leather or the smooth fabric, and you might not feel like getting up again any time soon. For domestic interior designers, the Ben Simhon showroom is a one-stop shopping destination. His latest collections include everything you ever needed to furnish your home – plus a lot of things you never knew you really, really needed.

DESIGN

Agas and Tamar [6]
43 Shabazi Street
Telephone (03) 5168421

The name of the shop means "pear and date," but it's actually taken from the last names of Einat Agasi and Tamar Harel-Klein, the designers who create and sell their unique jewelry from this location in Neve Tzedek. Agas and Tamar's designs are instantly recognizable among Tel Aviv's fashionistas – especially those with champagne taste and a budget to match. But these pieces are well worth the investment. One needn't be a jewelry expert to appreciate the clean lines, quality materials and understated luxury. The designers are inspired by antique jewelry, but their pieces are unmistakably classic and modern. This is also an excellent place to shop for unique wedding bands. Even if you don't plan to buy this time, stop by to obtain a copy of the catalogue. You'll be back.

CAFE

Cafe Mia [7]
55 Shabazi Street
Telephone (03) 5168793

Dolce Mia
55 Shabazi Street
Telephone (03) 5164647

Nestled in the heart of Neve Tzedek, Mia is one of Tel Aviv's most popular cafes – and deservedly so. The menu features excellent salads, sandwiches and the famous Israeli breakfast, all prepared with a unique and delicious fusion of Middle Eastern and European cuisines. Mia is a favorite hangout for both the local artist/bohemian community and visitors from abroad. The cozy decor is inviting and the service warm, friendly and responsive in typically laid-back Tel Aviv style. This is a lovely place to linger after a meal or over coffee, newspapers or a backgammon game, absorbing the local atmosphere. Next door, Dolce Mia offers beautiful homemade pastries and chocolate truffles. Only the very best ingredients are used – including gourmet chocolate from domestic boutique chocolateries.

CAFÉ & SUITES
Cafe Nina   [8]
29 Shabazi Street
Telephone (03) 5161767

Nina Suites
Telephone (052) 5084040

Located on Shabazi Street in Neve Tzedek, Cafe Nina is
both a popular cafe and a rather charming bed-and-breakfast.
The cafe on the ground floor is appealing for its cozy, old-
fashioned European decor, good coffee and nice selection of
well-prepared salads and sandwiches served on homemade
mini baguettes. The guest rooms upstairs are chic yet
comfortable, a perfect choice for visitors seeking an intimate
neighborhood atmosphere. Breakfast is included in the cost
of the room, the beach is five minutes' walk away and the
whole experience is very Tel Aviv meets Europe.

CAFE
Suzana [9]
9 Shabazi Street
Telephone (03) 5177580

Located in Neve Tzedek, opposite the Suzanne Dellal dance center, Suzana is practically a Tel Aviv institution. An enormous Ficus tree spreads its branches over the outdoor patio, shading diners as they enjoy the superb North African cuisine or the popular traditional Israeli breakfast. There is a cool breeze even during the hottest summer months, making this a peaceful place to linger over a perfectly brewed coffee. During the warm months, drinks and finger food are served on the rooftop bar starting from sunset, when a warm orange glow illuminates the horizon and the old buildings of Neve Tzedek.

Betty Ford [10]
48 Nachalat Binyamin Street
Telephone (03) 5100650

Betty Ford is a neighborhood restaurant and bar that manages successfully to be both chic and unpretentious. During the day it is a popular restaurant, serving homemade Middle Eastern specialties, such as couscous with stuffed vegetables. When night falls, the lights are dimmed and the early evening crowd comes for a light dinner accompanied by drinks and conversation. Later on, the DJ starts spinning and the beat picks up – and stays there into the small hours. For small groups there are tables in the patio out back and comfortable couches. The scene on the bar is hot on weekend nights.

Art Maroc [11]

38 Shabazi Street
Telephone (03) 5161326

As its name suggests, Art Maroc is purveyor of all things imported from Morocco. The shop on Shabazi Street is a bit reminiscent of a well-organized Ali Baba's cave, making it a very pleasant place to spend time browsing. It is packed with fabrics, lamps, ceramics and furniture, as well as many smaller items. Art Maroc has a wholesale outlet that deals in fabric and furniture for businesses. The owners offer suggestions for domestic interior design, as well as custom-made items created with materials purchased in Morocco.

Orca [12]

57 Nachalat Binyamin Street
Telephone (03) 5665505

Israeli critics are unanimous – Orca is among the best restaurants in the country. It has also been mentioned in several prestigious international publications, including The New York Times. Chef Eran Shroitman, a graduate of Le Cordon Bleu, fuses elements of French and Italian cuisine to create a traditional but surprising menu. Among the signature dishes are a single large ravioli filled with crab meat, goat's cheese and a whole egg yolk, and a thick, rich crab bisque. The wine list is impeccable, the service warm without being overly familiar and the surroundings are sleek and elegant.

RESTAURANT
Manta Ray [13]
Alma Beach, Tel Aviv promenade, opposite the Etzel Museum
Telephone (03) 5174773

Put together an attractive beachfront location, fresh seafood prepared with a distinctly Mediterranean flavor, casually friendly but very efficient waiters and you have the winning combination that has made Manta Ray one of the most popular restaurants in Tel Aviv. The food is reliably fresh and perfectly prepared, and the pounding of the waves provide a particularly pleasant backdrop to outdoor dining. A wide variety of mezze (appetizers), called "mezzitim" in Hebrew, are attractively presented on massive round platters, allowing patrons to choose the ones that look most appealing. Homemade flatbread is served as an accompaniment. For those who prefer meat to fish and seafood, there are several excellent choices. Granola and fresh fruit supplement the traditional Israeli breakfast, served daily from 9 A.M. until noon.

HOTEL
Dan Panorama [14]
Charles Clore Park
Telephone (03) 5190190
Reservation (03) 5202552

The Dan Panorama faces the beach on the southern tip of Tel
Aviv. Jaffa and Neve Tzedek are within easy walking distance,
so there is plenty to do, see, eat and buy. The Panorama is
popular with international business people because it offers
all the standard amenities expected of a luxury hotel, but at a
lower price. The rooms are comfortably furnished, and many
offer striking views of the beach and Old Jaffa. All have free
WiFi and cable television. The Charles Clore Park just opposite
is a very pleasant place to stroll and watch the sea.

FASHION

Babette [15]

31 Shabazi Street
Telephone (03) 5100534
2 Hei Beiyar, Kikar Hamedina
Telephone (03) 6963562

Babette is a charming boutique for children's clothing situated in the fashionable Neve Tzedek quarter. This is the ultimate mother's (or grandmother's) dream, with a wide variety of hip European designers for babies and older children. Ranging from the colorful and festive Oilily to the slightly hippie chic of Bon Point and the classic Petit Bateau, Babette is guaranteed to seduce buyers no matter what their taste. Other than children's clothing, there are T-shirts and bags for mothers and grandmothers as well as toys, linens, and accessories.

CAFE/DESIGN

Elya [16]
13 Amzaleg Street
Telephone (03) 5168836

Tucked away in a quiet, slightly hidden corner of Neve Tzedek, the entrance to Elya leads into a romantic courtyard with white iron patio furniture, a cherub fountain and colorful flowers blooming out of artfully placed planters. The water splashing gently into the fountain provides a peaceful accompaniment to a meal of lovingly prepared upscale cafe food, including a traditional Israeli breakfast that is served all day and a wide selection of excellent cakes and pastries. Inside, beyond the cafe area, there is a large shop selling exclusive imported home accessories, ranging from leather club chairs to bed sheets, Crabtree & Evelyn toiletries, a signature line of custom-made dishes and designer baby clothes. To complete the aesthetic pleasure, there is even a florist. At Elya, life feels rather beautiful.

Breakfast Club [17]

6 Rothschild Boulevard

Tucked away at the foot of Rothschild Boulevard, the Breakfast Club is currently the hottest nightspot in Tel Aviv. The late, late night scene at this uber-fashionable dance bar begins after midnight, when the doors open; it hits its stride around three o'clock in the morning and peaks when the other clubs and bars in the city close, about an hour later.If the bouncers judge you cool enough to be admitted to the smoky, dim interior, you'll have a pretty otherworldly Tel Aviv experience. The barmen keep the drinks flowing with impressive ease and some of the best DJs in town perform here. The decor is rather minimalist, with the only noticeable element a rather odd photo gallery – portraits of heroes and anti-heroes selected by the owners.

Armadilla [18]
38 Frankel Street
Telephone (03) 6818391

Like its slightly older and equally charming brother Armadillo, the recently opened Armadilla in Florentine is a friendly, unpretentious neighborhood bar with a lot of style and warmth. With its white-painted brick walls, long wooden bar and large, 1940s-style hanging light fixtures, Armadilla projects warmth and minimalism simultaneously. The bar shelves are well stocked and there are several draught beers that are relatively easy on the pocket. As at Armadillo, the food features homemade dishes like chopped liver and stuffed grape leaves. There are live music performances almost every evening.

Abraxas [19]
40 Lilienblum Street
Telephone (03) 5104435

Abraxas is one of the few bars in Tel Aviv that can be called an institution – even a legend. When Lilienblum Street began to develop into a center of Tel Aviv nightlife in the late 1990s, Abraxas led the way. Nearly a decade later, it still has its magic. Abraxas is one of the most popular places in the city to drink, listen to good music and soak up the sexy atmosphere. Its reputation is based on the owners' insistence on the best sound system, and on discovering talented new DJs who deserve to be promoted.

More of the best in the South end

RESTAURANT
Bellini
Italian on the square
6 Yechieli Street
Telephone (03) 5178486

RESTAURANT
Dinitz
Friday afternoon with the local papers
20 Gruzenberg Street
Telephone (03) 5161271

RESTAURANT
Kimmel
The Provencal place to eat
6 Hashachar Street
Telephone (03) 5161596

RESTAURANT
Nana Bar
Country village aesthetics
1 Ahad Ha'am Street
Telephone (03) 5161915

RESTAURANT
NG
For carnivores
6 Ahad Ha'am Street
Telephone (03) 5167888

NIGHT LIFE
Nanuchka
A must on the bar-hopper trail
28 Lilienblum Street
Telephone (03) 5162254

NIGHT LIFE
Bugsy
East Village meets Tel Aviv
26 Florentine Street
Telephone (03) 6813138

NIGHT LIFE
Norma Gin
Downtown bar for the heavy drinkers
23 Elifelet Street
Telephone (03) 6837383

NIGHT LIFE
Lenni's
Bohemian neighborhood bar
7 Vital Street
Telephone (03) 5186637

NIGHT LIFE
Satchmo
Whisky bar
6 Vital Street

NIGHT LIFE
Uzi Bach
A decent pick-up bar
30 Lilienblum Street
Telephone (03) 5162260

NIGHT LIFE
Lima Lima
For night owls
42 Lilienblum Street
Telephone (03) 5600924

NIGHT LIFE
Haoman 17
Mega nightclub
88 Abarbanel Street

CAFE
Taza d'oro
Friday afternoon jazz village
atmosphere
6 Ahad Ha'am Street
Telephone (03) 5166329

HOTEL
David Intercontinental
On the Mediterranean or when
Madonna is in town
12 Kaufman Street
Telephone (03) 7951111

SPA
Spa Moul Hayam
Relax by the beach
46 Herbert Samuel Street
Telephone (03) 5162818

Down town

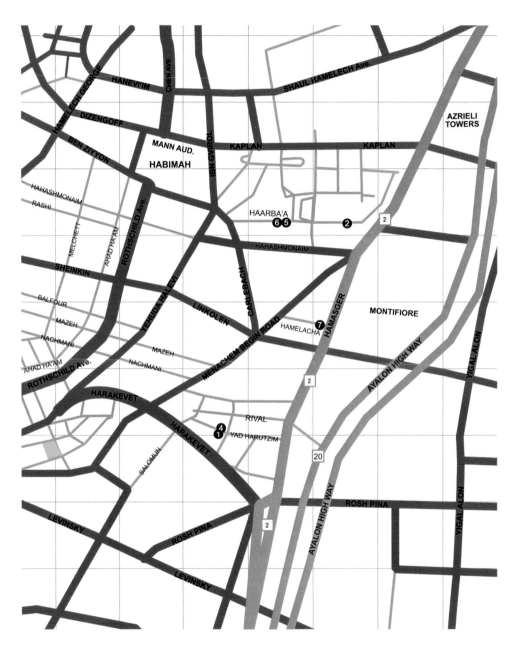

N

HANEVI'IM

CHEN AVE.

SHAUL HAMELECH Ave.

HAMELECH GEORGE

DIZENGOFF

BEN ZIYYON

MANN AUD.

IBN GVIROL

KAPLAN

KAPLAN

AZRIELI
TOWERS

HABIMAH

HAHASHMONAIM

RASHI

ROTHSCHILD Ave.

AHAD HA'AM

MELCHETT

HAARBA'A

6 5

2

2

SHEINKIN

BALFOUR

MAZEH

NACHMANI

AHAD HA'AM

ROTHSCHILD Ave.

YEHUDA HALEVI

LINKOLEN

CARLEBACH

MENACHEM BEGIN ROAD

HAHASHMONAIM

MAZEH

NACHMANI

HAMELACHA

7

HAMASGER

MONTIFIORE

AYALON HIGH WAY

YIGAL ALON

2

HARAKEVET

HARAKEVET

SALOMUN

RIVAL

4
1

YAD HARUTZIM

20

LEVINSKY

ROSH PINA

2

ROSH PINA

AYALON HIGH WAY

YIGAL ALON

LEVINSKY

300m

At first glance there doesn't seem to be much worth seeing or doing in this area of Tel Aviv. Yes, there's the observation tower on the 49th floor of the Azrieli Towers, but otherwise the area looks largely industrial in the south and solid, boring bourgeois in the north. Look a little closer, however, and you'll discover quite a lot. The industrial southern section is dotted with clubs and restaurants that popped up over the past few years, like flowers on a pile of manure. This area is probably not the first stop on a tourist's destination, but it is where locals "in the know" hang out. The northern section has a completely different appeal: There are several very good restaurants, cafes and shops, a bit of culture for those who crave it, and some nice green places for relaxing.

Yad Harutzim and Hamasger - The area around Yad Harutzim and Harakevet looks, to put it bluntly, rather charmless. Part of it is a maze of auto repair shops, interspersed with the highest concentration of office buildings in Tel Aviv. The multi-lane main roads – especially Menachem Begin Road – are crowded and noisy with traffic at all hours. The buildings appear to range from dilapidated old structures to lackluster commercial high rises. But there is much to explore and discover on foot. For amateur students of urban anthropology, a daytime walk around the Yad Harutzim/Hamasger area provides a fascinating picture of unstoppable urban development. This is Tel Aviv's newest commercial area and it is developing very rapidly. According to municipal law, all new high rises must be built along the Ayalon highway; but to avoid the creation of nocturnal ghost towns, the law allows for the creation of commercial and residential structures side by side. The result is an area that is always full of life, although it undergoes an interesting change in personality between conventional working hours and nights and weekends. Yad Harutzim Street really defines this area. Roughly comparable to New York's meat-packing district, it has undergone a complete renovation – with the Ayalon substituting for the Hudson River. About a dozen fashionable restaurants have sprung up over the past decade along Yad Harutzim, in the heart of the auto repair district. On weekdays the restaurants are packed to capacity with office workers, high-powered international business people, actors and musicians jockeying for tables. At night local residents, the beautiful and the glamorous (sometimes all wrapped up in one package) come to dine – many before embarking on a night of lounge bar and club crawling on nearby Hamasger Street. Hamasger is where some of the city's big names in nightlife are located – most prominently a mega-club called Dome. There are several smaller bars and clubs in close proximity, and they're all easy to find – just follow the crowds or listen for the music.And while you're exploring and discovering, remember that just over a decade ago this area was an utterly neglected, mostly forgotten, site of urban blight.

Hatikvah Market - Hatikvah means "hope" in Hebrew. Given that this neighborhood has, since it was established, been the home of Tel Aviv's more-or-less permanent underclass, its name is a bit ironic. For decades this most southeast neighborhood of Tel Aviv was a stronghold for North African and Yemenite immigrants. Recently many new immigrants from the former USSR have moved in – along with foreign workers from Eastern Europe, Africa and Southeast Asia. It is not unusual to see African women in traditional dress walking around Hatikvah Market. Despite its dead-end reputation, Hatikvah is a vibrant place to visit – particularly in the market area. There are many traditional Moroccan restaurants to sample, from sit-down establishments to no-frills outdoor stands where piles of grilled meat and pitta are served on plastic plates set on plastic tables. Almost everything is closed on Saturdays, but on Friday afternoons the atmosphere becomes frenetic as people shop and socialize on this first day of the weekend. Tourists don't know about Hatikvah, let alone visit it, so if you are looking for some really authentic, gritty urban atmosphere then Hatikvah Market is the place to soak it up.

The Azrieli Towers - Located on Menachem Begin Road where it meets Kaplan, the Azrieli Towers are probably the best-known – and certainly the most prominent – landmark in Tel Aviv. But in typical Israeli style, the towers were left incomplete for years. The original plans called for three structures – a circle, a triangle and a square. The circle and the square were completed, but the rusting iron metal girders of the unfinished triangle were left exposed to the elements for more than half a decade while the owners and the municipality argued about something or other. The issues were recently resolved, though, and work on the triangle is slated to be completed in the coming months. But even without the third tower, the Azrieli Towers are a fine sight at night, when they are all lit up. The standard American-style shopping mall on the first three floors of the circular tower has restaurants and a multiplex cinema, but there is nothing terribly exciting here. The main reason to visit is the observation platform on the 49th floor. The view really is stunning – extending up and down the Mediterranean Coast and eastward as far as Jordan on a clear day. Incidentally, the walled compound opposite the Azrieli Towers is in fact the headquarters of the IDF. The area just east of the army compound is the site of some old Templar Buildings that are currently undergoing renovation and restoration.

Montefiore - Located near Tel Aviv's biggest and busiest traffic intersection and dwarfed by the Azrieli Towers, the Montefiore neighborhood is one of the city's oldest. Once it was the center of the city's illicit gambling casinos and brothels, but today there is no sign of its nefarious past. Montefiore is quiet, subdued and rather characterless. Yehudit Boulevard, the central thoroughfare, is a pleasant street, lined with a few standard cafes that are patronized by people who work in the area – such as the staff of Yedioth Ahronoth newspaper and Shocken's "The City," weekend supplement, both of which have their offices in the area. Over the past five years there have been some signs of renewal in Montefiore. Starting in 2001 the municipality designated it a special status area – making it the only area in the city where artists' lofts and commercial space are allowed in the same buildings. And in fact many artists are moving in, taking advantage of the relatively low rents. In response, some enterprising developers saw Montefiore's housing potential and embarked on renovation projects to supply housing for middle-to-upper income bracket renters, but so far the area has not taken off in that direction.

Yehuda Halevy - Yehuda Halevy Street is a bit shabby looking, but it has several good restaurants, cafes and shops. If you're just strolling and you like Bauhaus architecture, it's well worth veering off onto some of the heavily treed side streets to look at some nice examples of classic Tel Aviv International-style apartment buildings.

Carlebach, Hahashmonaim, Haarba'a - The Cinematheque, the city's main art house cinema, is set in a leafy square on Sprinzak Street, where Hahashmonaim, Haarba'a and Carlebach intersect. The square is lined with benches and shaded by trees, making it a very pleasant place to sit. The cinema itself screens a wide variety of art-house films from all over the world, including cult films and Israeli underground hits. There is a bilingual schedule available in the lobby, which also houses a cafe in which live jazz is performed on Friday afternoons. Haarba'a is lined with good restaurants and is a popular destination for lunch and dinner. The Millenium Tower at the end of the street happens to be where former prime minister Ehud Barak has his office, but don't bother looking for his name on the buzzer because it isn't there. Security reasons, don'tcha know.

Hahashmonaim - Hahashmonaim is about to undergo a major change. For years one side was lined with falafel joints, shops and restaurants; the other was primarily a big, dirty open lot, occupied by the wholesale fruit and vegetable market. Recently the municipality decided to move the wholesale market to make room for a major luxury housing development. The decision was quite controversial, but the city got its way and the market was recently dug up by bulldozers. Construction is scheduled to start in late 2006 or 2007 – yet another indicator of how quickly Tel Aviv is developing.

Carlebach - Carlebach is named after Azriel Carlebach, the founding editor of Maariv newspaper. The Maariv building still stands in its original location. The street alternates between pleasant, in the area near the Cinematheque, and pleasantly ugly – where it borders the wholesale fruit and vegetable market. It's not a particularly distinguished thoroughfare, but if you find yourself there while wandering around the area of the Cinematheque, there are plenty of dining options. There are also a couple of clubs where live music of the sing-along variety, much beloved by the 50-plus crowd, is performed.

RESTAURANT
Coffee Bar [1]
13 Yad Harutzim Street
Telephone (03) 6889696

The Coffee Bar is a Tel Aviv institution. Don't let the name mislead you – it is the quintessential familiar bistro with a lively atmosphere in a casual, yet elegant, decor. The Coffee Bar was a maverick when it opened its doors 13 years ago in the grungy industrial area of Yad Harutzim. Its trendy, stylish fare was an instant success and it remains, more than a decade later, a place to see and be seen. The Coffee Bar pioneered the Tel Aviv bistro scene, becoming a leader in the culinary renaissance that took place during the 1990s. A few years ago the Coffee Bar spawned the celebrated Brasserie on Ibn Gvirol Street and recently the Bakery next door. For many, the Coffee Bar has become a metaphor for longevity and excellence. From early morning until late at night it hums with energy that evolves from a breakfast accompanied by classical music, to a busy power-lunch crowd, to a late night dinner crowd of regulars and insiders. Many share a fondness for the combination of upscale comfort food – such as sauteed chicken livers on silky mashed potatoes or a simple grilled Mediterranean fish. For those who prefer more sophisticated fare, the menu features bistro standards like confit de canard, seafood risotto or a perfect steak served with bone marrow. Daily specials are written on the large framed chalkboards. The friendly, efficient service is also one of the Coffee Bar's hallmarks.

RESTAURANT

Messa [2]
19 Haarba'a Street
Telephone (03) 6856859

Messa is the only Israeli restaurant featured in Conde Nast Traveler's list of the world's 80 Great New Restaurants. Chef Aviv Moshe has won praise from critics around the world for his unique, Provencal-influenced cuisine that is, he says, inspired by "memories from his mother's kitchen." He updates the menu constantly – depending on the season, locally available ingredients and his mood. Diners are invariably surprised and delighted by the imagination and depth of flavor in each dish. The richly varied drinks menu includes a variety of creative cocktails, expertly prepared and served by a professional staff. The intimate, dimly lit bar area is an attractive place to enjoy a pre-dinner drink and sample the imaginative offerings of the tasting menu. Messa has redefined chic dining in Israel with its striking decor. Designer Alex Mitlis expertly combines various seating arrangements with an imaginative interpretation of space that invites both intimacy and sociability. Wallpaper Magazine included Messa in its list of the 50 most beautiful restaurants in the world.

125

RESTAURANT
Chloélys
16 Abba Hillel Street, Ramat Gan
Telephone (03) 5759060

Chloélys is located amid the elegant towers of the diamond district in Ramat Gan, a bedroom community located just five minutes' drive from Tel Aviv. The distance is meaningless in physical terms and irrelevant for Tel Avivians, who quite rightly consider this elegant French-Mediterranean seafood restaurant to be a member of the city's pantheon of great dining establishments. Tel Aviv, Greater Tel Aviv - who cares? The point is to enjoy memorable food and good service in a stylish environment. Chloélys most certainly answers that description. Chef/owner Victor Gloger focuses on fish and seafood, fusing French and Mediterranean styles and ingredients to produce unfailingly impressive culinary delights. In addition to a wide variety of Mediterranean fish and seafood, Chloélys also imports unusual specimens from Paris' world-famous Rungis wholesale market twice weekly. The menu also includes entrees of meat that is aged on the premises. The extensive wine list includes over 200 hundred vintages chosen from the best local and international vineyards. There is also free parking, a boon for those who are accustomed to struggling with Tel Aviv's vehicle-clogged streets.

CAFE/BAKERY

Bakery [4]
13 Yad Harutzim Street
Telephone (03) 5371041

The pastries, cakes and breads served at the Coffee Bar are now available for purchase at the recently opened Bakery, located next door on Yad Harutzim. The Bakery is designed in the same style as the Coffee Bar, with marble counters and polished steel appliances creating a stylish environment. Everything is baked on the premises in an open kitchen, providing customers with a visual impression to accompany the seductive odors that make it nearly impossible to leave without buying just a bit more than you had intended. A branch of the Bakery will soon open next to the Brasserie, on Ibn Gvirol Street.

Onami [5]
18 Haarba'a Street
Telephone (03) 5621172

New sushi bars appear frequently in Tel Aviv, but stylish Onami, which opened about six years ago, is still considered among the very best. The chic, modern decor comprises walls painted in a warm shade of orange-red, rectangular dark wood tables and a curved sushi bar, where there is rarely an available seat during peak hours. At lunchtime Onami hums with quiet energy as patrons enjoy the business menu specials. At night the lights are dimmed to a flattering hue and the atmosphere becomes more intimate. The impeccably fresh and creative sushi, maki rolls and sashimi, beautifully presented on thick wood platters, are the biggest draws, but there are many other dishes – traditional and fusion – that are well worth trying. The agedashi tofu is a silky delight and the homemade soba noodles would do a Tokyo noodle shop proud. The well-trained waiting staff is friendly, sweet and efficient.

RESTAURANT
Tapeo [6]
16 Haarba'a Street
Telephone (03) 6240484

Tapeo combines flavors, service and atmosphere in ways that are guaranteed to please. Inspired by a Barcelona-style tapas bar, Tapeo is one of the city's most popular, stylish and happening gathering spots. A large, horseshoe-shaped bar dominates the spacious interior, which is pleasantly minimalist. Polished wood floors, tables lined up around the perimeter of the restaurant and bare walls painted dark orange and brown create a warm, intimate atmosphere that is perfectly conducive to leisurely socializing over beers, cocktails, wine and lots of tapas – delicious small portions that can be either a prelude to a meal or the meal itself. Tapeo is particularly appealing to Tel Avivians who, in typical Mediterranean style, love to socialize and enjoy drinking in the evening before a late dinner, but consider food to be an important accompaniment to alcohol. That's why Tapeo is buzzing with energy, every night of the week.

RESTAURANT
Pasta Mia
Italian for beginners
10 Wilson Street
Telephone (03) 5610189

RESTAURANT
Vince&Tamar
Nice people, good food
10 Hatzfira Street
Telephone (03) 6390407

RESTAURANT
Jos&Los
Jerusalem living-room scene
51 Yehuda Halevi Street
Telephone (03) 5606385

RESTAURANT
Dixie
When in the mood for chicken wings at 3am
120 Yigal Allon Street
Telephone (03) 6966123

RESTAURANT
Chimichanga
Santa Fe meets Tel Aviv
6 Kriminitzky Street
Telephone (03) 5613232

CAFE
Kremie
First coffee of the day
15 Kremie Street
Telephone (050) 7402838

CAFE
Tiferet
Coffee and art on the porch
81 Yehuda Halevi Street
Telephone (03) 5666164

RESTAURANT
Sergos [7]
8 Hamelacha Street
Telephone (03) 5615121

The warm, intimate decor of Sergos is reminiscent of a belle epoque Parisian cafe. It's very difficult to believe that this modern Tel Aviv interpretation of a classic bistro occupies a space that was once a car dealership. Located in rapidly up-and-coming down town Tel Aviv, near some of the city's trendiest clubs and lounge bars, Sergos is open 24 hours a day. The menu includes French bistro standards, Mediterranean-inspired dishes and daily specials that are based on a combination of season ingredients and the chef's inspiration. Guy Adler, the legendary barman who goes by the nickname Shemesh (Sun), serves up the cocktails with impressive expertise.

DESIGN
Habitat
Modern, modern, modern furniture
71 Ibn Gvirol Street
Telephone (03) 5279202

DESIGN
Villa Maroc
Silk Road aesthetics
110 Yehuda Halevi Street
Telephone (03) 5620401

DESIGN
Retro
Self-explanatory
123 Yehuda Halevi Street
Telephone (03) 6850663

NIGHT LIFE
The Dome
Wild nightclub
19 Hatzfira Street

NIGHT LIFE
Vox
Male-vox on Friday
2 Yagea Kapaim

NIGHT LIFE
Wallas
Dance bar
34 Rival Street

Jaffa

גן "ההודבתי"

וד
רים,

ביום האשון 18.5.66 בשעה
10 יקקים בגן מאיר סקס הבאת
ים של בני ילדים.

הילדים באים לגן בשעה 9.00
ים בגד לבן ומספחת לבנה
, בלי זר, את הגר הילדים
י בגן.

נחזורי בשעה 11.00

א למלוח סך 600 פרוטה עבוד
ת בהוצאות הקפס, הב.יעה

הג.ים מרזמנים.

בכבוד רב
יהודית

THE WAR IS OVER! GERMANY SURRENDERED! ALL SOLDIERS CEASE FIRE! THIS SURRENDER LEAFLET GUARANTEES EVERY GERMAN SOLDIER HIS LIFE!

DER KRIEG IST AUS! DEUTSCHLAND HAT SICH ERGEBEN! ALLE SOLDATEN STELLEN DAS SCHIESSEN EIN! DIESES ÜBERGABE MERKBLATT GARANTIERT JEDEM DEUTSCHEN SOLDATEN DAS LEBEN!

DWIGHT D. EISENHOWER

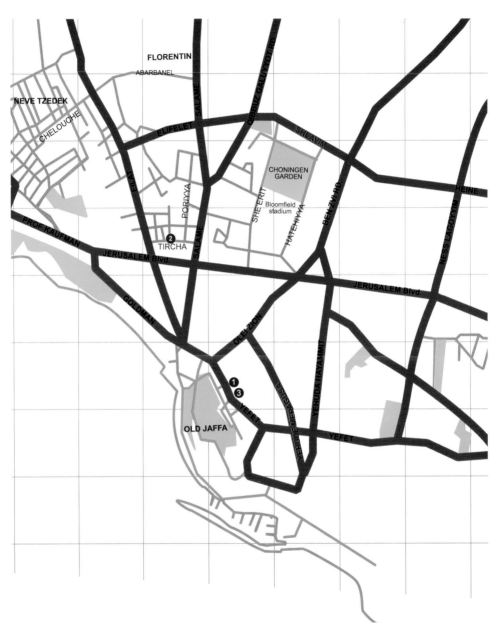

FLORENTIN

ABARBANEL

NEVE TZEDEK

CHELOUCHE

ELIFELET

SALAME

GIBBUZ GALUYOL RD.

SHLAVIM

CHONINGEN
GARDEN

EILAT

PORIYYA

SHE'ERIT

Bloomfield
stadium

BEN ZVI RD.

HA'TEHIYYA

HEINE

NESS LAGOYIM

PROF. KAUFMAN

JERUSALEM Blvd.

TIRCHA

SALAME

JERUSALEM Blvd.

GOLDMAN

OLEI ZION

YEHUDA HAYAMMIT

YEHUDA MEREGISA

YEFET

YEFET

OLD JAFFA

300m

Jaffa (Yafo in Hebrew, Yaffa in Arabic) can effectively be divided into two sections. Old Jaffa has a beautiful ancient port, restored historic sites, refurbished old houses and clusters of mostly upscale restaurants, galleries and shops. It is a major tourist attraction. The newer part of Jaffa is mostly residential, and has a heterogeneous population of Muslims, Christians and Jews. It is a culturally rich area with many beautiful old homes, green parks, lovely views, some good local restaurants and an authentic neighborhood feel.

History - Jaffa is one of the oldest port cities in the world, dating back to the Bronze Age. The city has a rich and violent history of conquest and re-conquest, destruction and reconstruction. It is mentioned in both the old and new testaments, and was used by King Solomon to import cedars from Tyre for the building of the First Temple. Subsequent rulers include the Arabs, starting from 636 C.E., the Crusaders five centuries later, the Ottomans, the Egyptian Mamluks and then the Ottomans again. When Napoleon conquered the city in 1799, he infamously drowned 2,000 Albanian prisoners in the harbor. All these historical events are noted and summarized on plaques at various sites in the refurbished port area. From the mid-19th century until the British conquest in 1917, the city was a thriving commercial hub of the Ottoman Empire. Its population of Muslims, Christians and Jews, who engaged in commerce, banking, fishing and manufacturing, swelled to the point of overcrowding by the beginning of the early 20th century. From the late 19th century until the 1920s, Jaffa was the headquarters of the modern Zionist movement in Israel. During the Arab Uprising of 1936-1939 there were several riots in Jaffa. As a result, most of the British and Jewish businesses moved to Tel Aviv. While neighboring Tel Aviv was originally established in 1909 as a suburb of Jaffa, it grew rapidly and eventually dwarfed the ancient city. In 1950, it was incorporated into Tel Aviv, creating the municipality of Tel Aviv-Jaffa. And yet, while the two cities are nominally one, they look and feel utterly different. This is partly, of course, because Jaffa is old and Tel Aviv is new. But it is also because Jaffa still has a heterogeneous population of Arabs and Jews living side-by-side; Tel Aviv has a large minority of non-Jews, but few Arabs live there.

The port city - The restored port city is clearly visible from the Tel Aviv beaches. Built on a hill overlooking the water, Old Jaffa juts out from the coastline and looks, from a distance, like a fortress – which it was, once. One of the nicest ways to approach Jaffa is to walk along the beachfront promenade, across the short wooden bridge that unofficially marks the place where it meets Tel Aviv – where the old city meets the new. This route will take you directly into the refurbished port area, with its lovely views and many historical sites that are clearly marked with signs and arrows.Notable sites include the Rock of Andromeda, the Zodiac Alleys, the Clock Tower – built in 1906 in honor of Sultan Abdul Hamid II – the Mahmoudia Mosque, St. Peter's Church, the Libyan Synagogue (now a museum) and the archaeological excavations at Jaffa Hill. Since they are all clustered close together, it is easy to see them all in a leisurely half day of exploring. There are many galleries, restaurants, museums and shops in old Jaffa. Since the area is small and well marked, there is really no need to list them here. You will inevitably discover them just by walking around the area. The restaurants facing the water are a bit pricey and sometimes a tad touristy, but not overly so. And given the view and the setting, it's easy to overlook these small drawbacks. Not all the restaurants overlook the water, however. Opposite the Clock Tower there are several upscale restaurants, cafes and bars tucked away on the side streets. These cater to Tel Aviv's fashionable and well-heeled crowd; if you are more interested in good food than the view, these places might be a better bet.The Tel Aviv municipality often hosts live musical performances in the square outside St. Peter's Church on summer nights. There are schedules posted and distributed around the square, or on the municipality website. The streets, named after the signs of the zodiac, are lined with galleries and artists' studios, as well as shops selling jewelry, Judaica and, surprisingly, not-too-tacky souvenirs.The very popular and very large flea market is just beyond the port. This is not the place to find Middle Eastern artifacts and souvenirs, though. The many shops and stands along the winding alleys sell an eclectic variety of goods that are more reminiscent of a European market than a Middle Eastern souq. Quite a few shops sell old furniture that looks like something your Austrian grandmother would have bought in Vienna, circa 1933. The hodgepodge of goods includes art, costume jewelry, crafts and quite a lot of stuff that looks rather like junk. You can bargain here to a certain extent, but unless you grew up in a Turkish bazaar don't expect to get too far with these seasoned, street-smart merchants.

Deeper into Jaffa - Few non-locals venture past the old port, deeper into Jaffa's residential neighborhoods. The only real exception to the rule is legendary Ali Karavan, popularly known as Abu Hassan's, which is frequently cited for the best hummus in Israel. Given that Israelis are completely obsessed with hummus, this is saying a lot. If you want to check out this 40-year-old hole-in-the wall, it's just down the hill on Dolphin Street. But get there early – by mid-afternoon the hummus is usually all gone.It's a pity the rest of Jaffa is so neglected by tourists, because it is a culturally and historically rich area. The restored old Ottoman homes in the old port are inhabited mostly by the rich, but Ajami and the rest of Jaffa are where the regular people live. There is also a beautiful beach – called Aliyah, or Ajami, Beach. This is really the only place in greater Tel Aviv where Jews and Arabs live side-by-side. Many point to Ajami as a particularly good example of peaceful co-existence.There are many beautiful old Ottoman homes in Ajami, especially around the area of Yefet, Toulouse and Kedem streets. There is some evidence of gentrification, but overall this is a laid-back, authentic neighborhood with a friendly atmosphere. Take your time walking around here – there are lots of interesting things to see. Yefet Street, near Toulouse, has a well-known ice cream shop that is open late at night and there is a pleasant cafe, called Paul's, right next door. The French ambassador's residence, built in the International style, is aptly located on Toulouse Street, facing the sea – just past the municipal Arab-Jewish community center, the green park and the Arab-Jewish school. Take a right on Kedem and walk along the beach; there are a couple of good, inexpensive seafood restaurants that are patronized by locals. There are also several nargileh bars, where local men (women are welcome, too) hang out to smoke, play backgammon and drink mint tea. The local mosque is a simple affair – the call to prayer is chanted by a real live person with a pleasantly modulated voice, rather than played from a scratchy recording via a public address system. The darker side of Jaffa is its reputation for criminal activity – mostly drug related. There are frequent turf wars between rival gangs that sometimes manifest themselves in shooting incidents. Since there has never been a case of an innocent bystander being caught in the crossfire, these incidents are rarely reported by the local media. Jaffa is also known for petty crime – mostly car and house break-ins. But none of this should scare visitors away. The streets are perfectly quiet and safe – particularly during the day – and in any case Israel is almost completely free of the type of violence that is so prevalent in major Western cities.

DESIGN

Workshop [1]

15 Yefet Street
Telephone (03) 5185928

The father-daughter design team Zvi and Hadas Shaham opened Workshop in 2004. Their eye-catching, eclectic designs include furniture, lamps, accessories and jewelry that are both modern and retro. Hadas is the jewelry designer. She uses silicon, rubber, concrete, gold and silver to create striking, modern pieces that are inspired by architecture. The attractive pieces successfully combine a look of delicacy and strength. In addition to creating his own modern, avant-garde style furniture, Zvi refurbishes carefully chosen retro pieces. They include furniture, light fixtures and accessories from the 1950s, '60s and '70s. Workshop is a lovely place in which to stop and browse during a stroll around Jaffa. It also deserves a special trip.

Poyke-African steaks & bar [2]
14 Tircha Street, Jaffa
Telephone (03) 6814622

The beautifully renovated old building in Jaffa that houses Poyke is a place of worship for stylish carnivores. Chef Ariel Cohen traveled around southern Africa to learn how to cook meat in a poyke, a traditional African cast iron cooking pot. He brought his knowledge back to Tel Aviv, added his own culinary ingenuity and voila – a unique new fusion food concept that combines beef, seafood, a wealth of inspired ingredients and unusual African spices. The results have earned rave reviews. Diners drool over his mustard seed-encrusted entrecote, the meat Cohen smokes himself and the legendary chocolate cake. Like almost everything else on the menu, the chocolate cake is prepared in a poyke – using a special method that Cohen developed himself. And it is spectacular. Even vegetarians will find themselves making a pilgrimage to Poyke just to eat that cake.

141

Cordelia [3]

1 Simtat Hazchuchit, Jaffa
Telephone (03) 5184668

Named for the loyal youngest daughter of Shakespeare's King Lear, Cordelia is indeed a palace worthy of a princess. Countless candles provide a warm, intimate light that illuminates the belle epoque interior, highlighting the sparkling wine glasses, the antique paintings, the mosaic tile floors and the shelves upon which stacks of wine bottles rest. The supremely romantic, soothing atmosphere enfolds diners as they experience some of the best, most imaginatively prepared cuisine in Israel. Celebrity Chef Nir Tzock, who has his own popular television cooking show and has published best-selling cookbooks, never fails to evoke smiles of pleasure from his diners – particularly with his famous degustation menu. He updates the seven-dish menu each month, with inspiration from classic French cuisine and a variety of fresh, local, seasonal ingredients. The result is an unforgettable fusion of French and Mediterranean flavors that consistently garners rave responses from critics and Cordelia's many loyal patrons. In addition to Cordelia, Tzock also owns Jaffa Bar and Bistro Noa – all housed in the same building complex. Like Cordelia, they are warm, romantic places to gather for an evening of eating and drinking.

More of the best in Jaffa

RESTAURANT
Yoezer Wine Bar
Gem in Jaffa
2 Yoezer Ish Habira Street
Telephone (03) 6839115

RESTAURANT-HUMMUS
Ali Karavan
By far the best hummus in town
1 Dolphin Street
Telephone (03) 6280387

CAFE
Pua
Eclectic in the flea market
3 Rabbi Yochanan Street
Telephone (03) 6823821

NIGHT LIFE
Saluna
Art exhibits in a downtown bar
17 Tircha Street
Telephone (03) 5181719

NIGHT LIFE
Dungeon
S&M – need we say more?
14 Kikar Kedumim Street
Telephone (03) 5180642

HOTEL
Andromed hill
Apartment hotel
3 Luie paster Street
Telephone (03) 6838448

Contact

Galleries

Alon Segev Gallery
23 Shaul Hamelech Street
Telephone (03) 6090769
www.alonsegevgallery.com

Bauhaus Center
99 Dizengoff Street
Telephone (03) 5220249
www.bauhaus-center.com

Bineth Gallery
15 Frishman Street
Telephone (03) 5238910
www.binethgallery.com

Bernard Gallery
170 Ben Yehuda Street
Telephone (03) 5270547

Braverman Gallery
81 Yehuda Halevi Street
Telephone (03) 5666162
www.byartprojects.com

Chelouche Gallery
5 Chissin Street
Telephone (03) 5289713

Contemporary Art Room
11 Gotlieb Street
Telephone (03) 5222402

Dan Gallery
74 Ben Yehuda Street
Telephone (03) 5243968
www.finegallery.com

Dvir Gallery
11 Nachum Street
Telephone (03) 6043003
www.dvirgallery.com

Engel Gallery
26 Gordon Street
Telephone (03) 5225637
www.engel-art.co.il

Farkash Gallery
5 Mazal Dagim Street
Telephone (03) 6834741
www.farkash-gallery.com

Givon Gallery
35 Gordon Street
Telephone (03) 5225427

Gordon Gallery
95 Ben Yehuda Street
Telephone (03) 5240935
www.gordongallery.com

Hagar Art Gallery
99 Yefet Street
www.hagar-gallery.com

Julie M.Gallery
7 Glikson Street
Telephone (03) 5253389
www.juliem.com

Kibbutz Gallery
25 Dov Hoz Street
Telephone (03) 5232533
www.kibutzgallery.org.il

Nelly Aman Gallery
26 Gordon Street
Telephone (03) 5232003

Noga Gallery
60 Ahad Ha'am Street
Telephone (03) 5660123
www.nogagallery.co.il

Rosenfeld Gallery
147 Dizengoff Street
Telephone (03) 5229044
www.rg.co.il

Sommer Gallery
13 Rothschild Boulevard
Telephone (03) 5166400
www.sommergallery.com

Stern Gallery
30 Gordon Street
Telephone (03) 5246303
www.sternart.com

Tal Esther Gallery
101 Yehuda halevi Street
Telephone (03) 5601807
www.talesthergallery.com

Tova Osman Gallery
100 Ben Yehuda Street
Telephone (03) 5227687

33 Gallery
33 Yehuda Halevi Street
Telephone (03) 5165418
www.gallery33.co.il

Museums

Ben-Gurion House
17 Ben-Gurion Avenue
Telephone (03) 5221010

Diaspora Museum
Tel Aviv University campus
Telephone (03) 6408000
www.bh.org.il

Bialik House
22 Bialik Street
Telephone (03) 5254530

Eretz Israel Museum
2 Haim Levanon Street
Ramat Aviv
Telephone (03) 6415244
www.eretzmuseum.org.il

Etzel Museum 1947-1948
South Herbert Samuel Promenade
Telephone (03) 5172044

Haganah Museum
23 Rothschild Boulevard
Telephone (03) 5608624

Hapalmach Museum
10 Haim Levanon Street
Ramat Aviv
Telephone (03) 6436393

Helena Rubinstein Pavilion
6 Tarsat Avenue
Telephone (03) 5287196

House of the Bible
16 Rothschild Boulevard
Telephone (03) 5166393

Ilana Gur Museum
4 Mazal Dagim Street
Telephone (03) 6837676
www.ilanagur.com

Independence Hall
16 Rothschild Boulevard
Telephone (03) 5173942

Israel Army Museum
35 Eilat Street
Telephone (03) 5161346

Jabotinsky Institute
38 King George Street
Telephone (03) 5284001

Nachum Gutman Museum
21 Rokach Street
Telephone (03) 5161970
www.gutmanmuseum.co.il

Rokach House
36 Shimon Rokach Street
Neve Tzedek
Telephone (03) 5168042
www.rokach-house.co.il

Rubin House
14 Bialik Street
Telephone (03) 5255961
www.rubinmuseum.org.il

Shalom Alechem House
4 Berkovich Street
Telephone (03) 6956513

Tel Aviv Museum of Art
27 Shaul Hamelech Avenue
Telephone (03) 6077000
www.tamuseum.com

Yair House Museum
8 Avraham Stern Street
Telephone (03) 6820288

Cultural Centers

Beit Ariela Cultural Center
25 Shaul Hamelech Street
Telephone (03) 6910141

Beit Lessin Theater
101 Dizengoff Street
Telephone (03) 7255333

Camel Comedy Club
52 Hakongress Street
Telephone (03) 6393434

Gesher Theater
9 Jerusalem Avenue
Telephone (03) 6813131

**Habima -The National
Theater**
2 Tarsat Avenue
Telephone (03) 5266666

**The Mann Auditorium
The Israeli Philharmonic**
1 Huberman Street
Telephone (03) 6290193

Hasimta Theater
8 Mazal Dagim Street
Telephone (03) 6812126

**Suzanne Dellal Center for
Dance & Theater**
5 Yechieli Street
Telephone (03) 5105656

The Cameri Theater
30 Leonardo da Vinci Street
Telephone (03) 6060960

The Opera House
19 Shaul Hamelech Street
Telephone (03) 6927700

Tmuna Theater
8 Shonchino Street
Telephone (03) 5629462

Tzavta
30 Ibn Gvirol Street
Telephone (03) 6950156

**Zionist Organization of
America House**
26 Ibn Gvirol Street
Telephone (03) 6959341

Index

Restaurants

Agadir - Bar Burger   [32]
3 Hata'arucha Street,
Tel Aviv Port
Telephone (03) 5444045
Fax   (03) 5462381
2 Nachalat Binyamin Street
Telephone (03) 5104442
www.agadir.co.il

Ali Karavan hummus
1 Dolpfin Street
Telephone (03) 6280387

Barbunia Bar
192 Ben Yehuda Street
Telephone (03) 5240961

Bellini
6 Yechieli Street
Telephone (03) 5178486

Boya
3 Hata'arucha Street, Tel Aviv port
Telephone (03) 5446166

Brasserie   [46]
70 Ibn Gvirol Street
Telephone (03) 6967111
Fax   (03) 6096053

Cafe Noir   [78]
43 Ahad Ha'am Street
Telephone (03) 5663018
Fax   (03) 6293841

Cantina   [77]
71 Rothschild Boulevard
Telephone (03) 6205051
Fax   (03) 6202090
www.rest.co.il/cantina

Carmella bistro   [96]
14 Rambam Street
Telephone (03) 5161417
Fax   (03) 5161368
bistro@zahav.net.il
www.rest.co.il/carmella

Chimichanga
6 Kriminitzky Street
Telephone (03) 5613232

Chloélys [126]
16 Abba Hillel Street,
Ramat Gan
Telephone (03) 5759060
Fax   (03) 5759070
www.rest.co.il/chloelys

Coffee Bar   [122]
13 Yad Harutzim Street
Telephone (03) 6889696
Fax   (03) 6394541

Comme il faut   [22] Restaurant
Bait Banamal, Hanger 26,
Tel Aviv Port
Telephone (03) 5449211
Fax   (03) 5449187

Cordelia   [142]
1 Simtat Hazchuchit, Jaffa
Telephone (03) 5184668
Fax   (03) 5183418
www.cordelia.co.il

Dinitz
20 Gruzenberg Street
Telephone (03) 5161271

Dita
45 Rothschild Boulevard
Telephone (03) 5604222

Dixie
120 Yigal Allon Street
Telephone (03) 6966123

El Pastio
27 Ibn Gvirol Street
Telephone (03) 5251166

Giraffe   [51]
49 Ibn Gvirol Street
Telephone (03) 6916294
Fax   (03) 6091806

Jos&Los
51 Yehuda Halevi Street
Telephone (03) 5606385

Kimel
6 Hashachar Street
Telephone (03) 5161596

Kyoto Tel Aviv   [72]
31 Montefiore Street
Telephone (03) 5661234
Fax   (03) 5601486

Lilit
2 Dafna Street
Telephone (03) 6091331

Manta Ray   [106]
Alma Beach,
Tel Aviv promenade,
Opposite Etzel Museum
Telephone (03) 5174773
Fax   (03) 5108891
www.mantaray.co.il

Meat Bar
52 Chen Boulevard
Telephone (03) 6956276

Messa   [124]
19 Haarba'a Street
Telephone (03) 6856859
Fax   (03) 6858001
www.messa.co.il

Moses
35 Rothschild Boulevard
Telephone (03) 5664949

Moul Yam   [26]
Hangar 24, Tel Aviv Port
Telephone (03) 5469920
Fax   (03) 5469940
www.mulyam.com

Nana Bar
1 Ahad Ha'am Street
Telephone (03) 5161915

NG
6 Ahad Ha'am Street
Telephone (03) 5167888

Onami [128]
18 Haarba'a Street
Telephone (03) 5621172
Fax   (03) 5620974

Orca [105]
57 Nachalat Binyamin Street
Telephone (03) 5665505
www.rest.co.il/orca

Orna&Ella [76]
33 Sheinkin Street
Telephone (03) 6204753
Fax   (03) 5283376

Pasta Mia
10 Wilson Street
Telephone (03) 5610189

Pastis
70 Rothschild Boulevard
Telephone (03) 5250773

Poyke [141]
14 Tircha Street, Jaffa
Telephone (03) 6814622
Fax   (03) 6814622
www.poyke.com

Pronto [74]
26 Nachmani Street
Telephone (03) 5660915
www.pronto.co.il

Raphael
87 Hayarkon Street
Telephone (03) 5226464

Sergos [130]
8 Hamelacha Street
Telephone (03) 5615121
Fax   (03) 5611491
www.rest.co.il/sergos

Stephan Brown
99 Allenby Street
Telephone (03) 5604725

Tapeo [129]
16 Haarba'a Street
Telephone (03) 6240484

The Thai House
8 Bograshov Street
Telephone (03) 5178568

Toto
4 Berkovich Street
Telephone (03) 6935151

Vince&Tamar
10 Hatzfira Street
Telephone (03) 6390407

Yoezer Wine bar
2 Yoezer Ish Habira Street
Telephone (03) 6839115

Cafes

Bakery [127]
13 Yad Harutzim Street
Telephone (03) 5371041

Batcho
85 King George Street
Telephone (03) 5289753

Bookworm [58]
9 Kikar Rabin Street
Telephone (03) 5298490
Fax   (03) 5298490
www.bookworm.co.il

Cafe Ashtor [33]
37 Basel Street
Telephone (03) 5465318

Cafe Bialik
2 Bialik Street
Telephone (03) 6200832

Cafe Masaryk
12 Masaryk Square
Telephone (03) 5272411

Cafe Mia [101]
55 Shabazi Street
Telephone: (03) 5168793

Cafe Michal [33]
230 Dizengoff Street
Telephone (03) 5230236

Cafe Nina [102]
29 Shabazi Street
Telephone: (03) 5161767
elizanina@012.net.il

Cafe Noach
93 Ahad Ha'am Street
Telephone (03) 6293799

Cafe Tamar
57 Sheinkin Street
Telephone (03) 6852376

Dolce Mia [101]
55 Shabazi Street
Telephone: (03) 5164647

Elkalai
1 Elkalai Street
Telephone (03) 6041260

Elya [109]
13 Amzaleg Street
Telephone (03) 5168836
Fax   (03) 5165086
www.elyadesign.co.il

Emily
30 Basel Street
Telephone (03) 5462714

Hurkanos
187 Ibn Gvirol Street
Telephone (03) 5467869

Idelson 10
252 Ben Yehuda Street
Telephone (03) 5444154

Gabriel [81]
42 Montefiore Street
Telephone (03) 5667020
Fax (03) 5604993
www.gabrieltlv.co.il

Ginzburg
55 Ahad Ha'am Street
Telephone (03) 5608070

Kremie
15 Kremie Street
Telephone (050) 7402838

Lechem Erez
52 Ibn Gvirol Street
Telephone (03) 6965680

Libra
120 Ben Yehuda Street
Telephone (03) 5298764

Lilush
73 Frishman Street
Telephone (03) 5379354

Loveat
1 Barzilai Street
Telephone (03) 5666696

Meshulash
168 Dizengoff Street
Telephone (03) 5236734

Moving
308 Dizengoff Street
Telephone (03) 5444434

Pua
3 Rabbi Yochanan Street
Telephone (03) 6823821

Shine
38 Shlomo Hamelech Street
Telephone (03) 5276186

Suzana [103]
9 Shabazi Street
Telephone (03) 5177580
www.rest.co.il/suzana

Tiferet
81 Yehuda Halevi Street
Telephone (03) 5666164

Zorik
4 Yehuda Hamaccabi Street
Telephone (03) 6048858

Night life

Abraxas [111]
40 Lilienblum Street
Telephone (03) 5104435

Armadilla [111]
38 Frenkel Street
Telephone (03) 6818391

Armadillo [79]
51 Ahad Ha'am Street
Telephone (03) 6205573

Bugsy
26 Florentine Street
Telephone (03) 6813138

Betty Ford [104]
48 Nachalat Binyamin Street
Telephone (03) 5100650

The Breakfast Club [110]
6 Rothschild Boulevard

The Dome
19 Hatzfira Street

Dungeon
14 Kikar Kedumim Street
Telephone (03) 5180642

Fetish
48 King George Street

Galina
Hangar 19, Tel Aviv Port
Telephone (03) 5445553

Helena [75]
4-a Tarsat Avenue, Jacob's Garden
Telephone (03) 5289289

Lenni's
7 Vital Street
Telephone (03) 5186637

Molly Bloom's
2 Mendele Street
Telephone (03) 5221558

Nanuchka
28 Lilienblum Street
Telephone (03) 5162254

Norma Gin
23 Elifelet Street
Telephone (03) 6837383

Saluna
17 Tircha Street
Telephone (03) 5181719

Satchmo
6 Vital Street

Shalvata
Tel Aviv Port
Telephone (03) 5441279

Shoshana Johnson
97 Allenby Street
Telephone (03) 5607443

Uzi Bach
30 Lilienblum Street
Telephone (03) 5162260

Vox
2 Yagea Kapaim

Wallas
34 Rival Street

Whisky a Go Go [34]
3 Hata'arucha Street, Tel Aviv Port
Telephone (03) 5440633

Design

Agas and Tamar [100]
43 Shabazi Street
Telephone (03) 5168421
Fax (03) 5166876
www.agasandtamar.com

Arik Ben Simhon [98]
110 Nachalat Binyamin
Telephone (03) 6837865
absimhon@bezeqint.net

Art Maroc [105]
38 Shabazi Street
Telephone (03) 5161326
Artmaroc@zahav.net.il

Blue Bandana [31]
52 Hei Beiyar, Kikar Hamedina
Telephone: (03) 6021686
bbandana@netvision.net.il

Carousel
27 Rothschild Boulevard
Telephone (03) 5603750

Elya [109]
13 Amzaleg Street
Telephone (03) 5168836
Fax   (03) 5165086
www.elyadesign.co.il

Gabriel [80]
42 Montefiore Street
Telephone (03) 5667020
Fax   (03) 5604993
www.gabrieltlv.co.il

Habitat
71 Ibn Gvirol Street
Telephone (03) 5279202

Kastiel & Sons [94]
Design Center
9 Wolfson Street
Telephone: (03) 6836334
Kastiel@kastiel.com

Orit Ivshin [97]
53 Shabazi Street
Telephone: (03) 5160811
www.oritivshin.com

Retro
123 Yehuda Halevi Street
Telephone (03) 6850663

Sami D. [97]
56 Shabazi Street
Telephone (03) 5164968
samyd_il@netvision.net.il

Shay Lahover [24]
203 Dizengff Street
Telephone: (03) 5233887
www.shay-lahover.com

Tollman's [53]
Gan Ha'ir, 71 Ibn Gvirol Street
Telephone: (03) 5223236
www.tollmans.co.il

Villa Maroc
110 Yehuda Halevi Street
Telephone (03) 5620401

Workshop [140]
15 Yefet Street
Telephone: (03) 5185928
www.workshop.co.il

Yael Herman Gallery [27]
211 Dizengoff Street
Telephone: (03) 5221816
Mobile: 052 3676647
Yael_he@netvision.net.il

Fashion

Alma
9 Ba'alei Melacha Street
Telephone (03) 6200145

Babette [108]
31 Shabazi Street
Telephone (03) 5100534
Fax   (03) 5100534
2 Hei beiyar, Kikar Hamedina
Telephone (03) 6963562

Banot [28]
212 Dizengoff Street
Telephone (03) 5291175
40 Sheinkin Street
Telephone (03) 5281796
Lulu-l@zahav.net.il

Comme il faut [22]
Bait Banamal, Hanger 26, Tel Aviv Port
Telephone (03) 6025530
Fax   (03) 6041025
www.comme-il-faut.com

Daniella Lehavi [30]
34 Basel Street
Telephone (03) 5440573
35 Sheinkin Street
Telephone (03) 6294044
www.daniellalehavi.com

Delicatessen [80]
4 Barzilai Street
Telephone (03) 5602297
www.delicatessen-studio.com

Dina Glass
35 Nachmani Street
Telephone (03) 5602493

Dorin Frankfurt
164 Dizengoff Street
Telephone (03) 5270374

Doron Ashkenazi
187 Dizengoff Street
Telephone (03) 5272679

Fabiani [29]
280 Dizengoff Street
Telephone (03) 6025569
Fax   (03) 5234443
diana@diana-churges.com

Frau Blau [80]
8 Hachashmal Street
Telephone (03) 5601735
www.fraublau.com

Frida [28]
190 Dizengoff Street
Telephone (03) 5225151
www.frida.co.il

Gertrud [49]
225 Dizengoff Street
Telephone (03) 5467747
Fax   (03) 5440949
Gertrud@gmail.com

Ido Recanati
13 Malchei Israel Street
Telephone (03) 5298481

Katomenta [53]
173 Dizengoff Street
Telephone (03) 5279899
Fax   (03) 5229758
www.katomenta.com

Kedem Sasson
213 Dizengoff Street
Telephone (03) 5232981
www.maisonrouge-homme.com

Kisim [79]
8 Hachashmal Street
Telephone (03) 5604890
Fax   (03) 5604896
www.kisim.com

Mayu [48]
7 Malchei Israel, Kikar Rabin
Telephone (03) 5273992
61 Ussishkin, Ramat Hasharon
Telephone (03) 5499033
mayu@012.net.il

Nait
10 Mikve Israel Street
Telephone (03) 5600402

Naama Bezalel
40 Sheinkin Street
Telephone (03) 6293938

Ronen Chen [52]
155 Dizengoff Street
Telephone (03) 5275672
49 Sheinkin Street
Telephone (03) 5280360
www.ronenchen.com

Metzada Ba'kikar [25]
60 Hei beiyar, Kikar Hamedina
Telephone (03) 5447766
Fax   (03) 5447733

Sarah Brown
162 Dizengoff Street
Telephone (03) 5299902

Shani Bar
3 Mikve Israel Street
Telephone (03) 5605981

Shufra shoes
108 Dizengoff Street
Telephone (03) 5247274

Yossef
213 Dizengoff Street
Telephone (03) 5298991

Hotels & Spas

Andromeda Hill
3 Louis Pasteur Street
Telephone (03) 6838448

Dan Panorama [107]
Charles Clore Park
Telephone (03) 5190190
Reservation (03) 5202552
www.danhotels.co.il

Dan Tel Aviv [56]
99 Hayarkon Street
Telephone (03) 5202525
Reservations (03) 5202552
www.danhotels.co.il

Hilton Tel Aviv
Independence Garden
Telephone (03) 5202222

Nina Suites [102]
29 Shabazi Street
Telephone (052) 5084040
elizanina@012.net.il

Prima Tel Aviv [50]
105 Hayarkon Street
Telephone (03) 5206666
Fax   (03) 5237242
www.prima.co.il

Sheraton Tel Aviv [57]
115 Hayarkon Street
Telephone (03) 5211111
Fax   (03) 5233322
www.sheraton-telaviv.co.il

Spa coola [22]
Bait Banamal, Hanger 26
Tel Aviv Port
Telephone (03) 5444462
Fax   (03) 5444974
www.coola.co.il

Spa Moul Hayam
46 Herbert Samuel Street
Telephone (03) 5162818

Villa Spa
10 Yehuda Hamacabi Street
Telephone (03)5460608

Book Shops

Bookworm [58]
9 Kikar Rabin Street
Telephone (03) 5298490
Fax   (03) 5298490
www.bookworm.co.il

Polak
36 King George Street
Telephone (03) 5288613

Contents

Producer and editor: Dalit Nemirovsky
Art and graphic design: Lora Rozenberg
Research and texts: Lisa Goldman
Photography: Natan Dvir
Production assistant: Moria Goldstein
Pre-print: Hadas Tagor

**Special thanks to Mati Broudo
for making this book possible**

Although every effort has been made to ensure that the information
in this book is as up-to-date and as accurate as possible at the time of
going to press, some details are liable to change.

First Published in Israel in 2006 by
Crossfields Publishing, 123 Rothschild Ave, Tel Aviv

Israeli Library Cataloguing-in-Publication Data
A Catalogue record for this book is available
from the Israeli Library.

ISBN 965-90997-0-3

Printed in Israel by Keterpress Enterprises